Oxford School Shakespeare

As You Like It

edited by

Roma Gill
M.A. *Cantab*. B.Litt. *Oxon*.

Oxford University Press
Oxford   Toronto   Melbourne

Oxford University Press, Walton Street, Oxford OX2 6DP
Oxford   New York
Athens   Auckland   Bangkok   Bombay
Calcutta   Cape Town   Dar es Salaam   Delhi
Florence   Hong Kong   Istanbul   Karachi
Kuala Lumpur   Madras   Madrid   Melbourne
Mexico City   Nairobi   Paris   Singapore
Taipei   Tokyo   Toronto

and associated companies in
Berlin   Ibadan

Oxford is a trade mark of Oxford University Press

© Oxford University Press 1977
First published 1977
Reprinted 1978, 1985, 1988, 1989, 1991, 1992
This revised edition first published 1994
Reprinted 1994

ISBN 0 19 831979 7

Illustrations by Coral Mula

Cover photograph by Donald Cooper (Photostage)
shows Adam Kotz as Orlando and Fiona Shaw
as Rosalind in the Old Vic's 1989 production of
As You Like It.

Oxford School Shakespeare

edited by Roma Gill

A Midsummer Night's Dream

Romeo and Juliet

As You Like It

Macbeth

Julius Caesar

The Merchant of Venice

Henry IV Part I

Twelfth Night

The Taming of the Shrew

Othello

Hamlet

King Lear

Printed in Great Britain at the University Press, Cambridge

Contents

For Carolyn

As You Like It and the actors

As You Like It! The title of the play forbids any critic to say that his interpretation is the right one, and the only one. I can therefore tell you simply what *I* find, and then you can take or leave my opinion *as you like it*. In what follows, I am thinking on paper, giving you a running commentary as I read the play. But first, I want to say a few words about Shakespeare's involvement with the theatre, because it is especially relevant to this play.

In every way, Shakespeare was a man of the theatre. He wrote for it, he acted in it, and, as a shareholder in the playhouse for which he wrote, he made a profit from it. As a businessman, he needed to make sure that the plays which he (as a dramatist) wrote would be financially successful. As an actor, one of the company known as The Lord Chamberlain's Men, he knew the talents of his fellow-actors, and could write plays which would show these talents at their best.

As You Like It was a perfect play for The Lord Chamberlain's Men in 1599. They were performing in a newly built theatre, the Globe, and Jaques' metaphor, 'All the world's a stage' (2, 7, 139) was a good advertisement. There were two boy actors (who played the women's parts) in the company: one was tall and fair, the other short and dark. We know this, not from any theatre programmes (for there were none) but from plays which Shakespeare wrote at this time. Both *A Midsummer Night's Dream* and *Much Ado About Nothing* have parts which demand such actors. In *As You Like It* Oliver is given a description of the brother and sister that he must look for:

> The boy is fair,
> Of female favour, and bestows himself
> Like a ripe sister. The woman low,
> And browner than her brother.   (4, 3, 85–8)

Another actor in the company was the comedian, Robert Armin. Armin's own writings show that he was a witty, sophisticated comedy actor, and dramatic records tell us that he played other parts similar to that of Touchstone in this play. Shakespeare also perhaps intended him to play Amiens (the two roles can be doubled) because he sang well.

There are many songs in the plays of this period: the dramatic company must have had several good singers. In *As You Like It* the songs are appropriate for the play, almost making it a 'musical comedy'. They serve practical purposes as well. In *Act 2*, Scene 7, it is necessary for Orlando to explain to Duke Senior why he has come to the Forest of Arden. To avoid boring the audience with what they already know, Orlando whispers to the duke at the back of the stage, whilst Amiens sings to entertain the duke's followers—and the audience. Near the end of the play, Rosalind tells the lovers 'To-morrow meet me all together' (5, 2, 114). A song is sung by two pages, which occupies almost the whole of *Act 5*, Scene 3; then, in Scene 4, the meeting takes place. A day has passed whilst the song was being sung.

We can see from *As You Like It* that Shakespeare knew how to exploit the resources of his company. I think it is helpful to remember this, because sometimes, when the play is being read, there are passages which seem irrelevant: they neither advance the plot nor develop the characters, and they could be said to have no *dramatic* function. But they often have a *theatrical* function. Such a passage is Jaques' famous speech in *Act 2*, Scene 7, which begins (line 139)

> All the world's a stage,
> And all the men and women merely players.

This speech gives Orlando time to find Adam and bring him back to the duke's feast; it also gives the actor playing Jaques an opportunity to display his professional skill. *As You Like It* suffers more than most of Shakespeare's plays when it is read in a book instead of being performed on a stage.

When the play is acted, the different characters are colourful and alive; the words they speak and the ideas they express appear to come from their individual natures and the situations in which they find themselves. On the page, there is no colour and no individuality. The reader is aware that the plot is thin, and that the characters are mostly very easy to understand. Rosalind dominates the play in performance, with her charm and gaiety; the reader of the play is not so easily seduced by her.

A great effort of imagination is required from the reader, who must first of all attempt to see the play with his mind's eye. In *As You Like It* Shakespeare presents a number of themes which were of particular interest to the Elizabethans; members of the audience would leave the Globe intellectually stimulated and ready to continue discussing the play's themes amongst themselves. The topics are not always *immediately* relevant to twentieth-century readers, yet when we make the effort we can see that, for instance, the debate on satire and the satirist (2, 7, 36–87) is as appropriate now as it was then. We need not dismiss the ideas, just because they are presented in Elizabethan costume; the ideas give strength to the plot. Because the ideas are relevant to the facts of Elizabethan life and culture, they help us to forget that the plot is an absurd fiction.

Source, Date, and Text

A book gave Shakespeare the foundations of his play. Thomas Lodge's novel *Rosalynde* (published in 1590) provided the intertwined plots, and suggested all the characters except Touchstone and Jaques. The play begins, as the novel does, with the plot concerning three brothers.

As You Like It must have been written in the last years of the sixteenth century. The actor who played Touchstone, Robert Armin, did not join Shakespeare's theatrical company until 1599. The play was entered (for registration of copyright) in the Stationers' Register in 1600, but it was not published until 1623, when it appeared in the great collection of Shakespeare's plays known as the First Folio.

Leading characters in the play

Duke Senior   the rightful duke, who has been deposed by his younger brother. He lives in the Forest of Arden, with a number of lords who have rejected court life.

Duke Frederick   the younger brother of Duke Senior. Having deposed his brother, and usurped the title 'duke', he now rules over the court. He is moody and suspicious, and feared rather than loved by those who serve him.

Rosalind   daughter of Duke Senior. She is the most attractive and important character in the play. Although for much of the time she dresses as a boy (calling herself Ganymede), she is very feminine, especially when she is in love with Orlando. She is very quick-witted.

Celia   daughter of Duke Frederick, and Rosalind's cousin. She is not so dominant as Rosalind, but is still clever and attractive. She is also loyal to her cousin, and when Rosalind is banished by Duke Frederick, Celia accompanies her cousin to the Forest. When she is disguised as a country girl, she takes the name Aliena.

Oliver and Orlando de Boys   These two brothers, sons of Sir Rowland de Boys, are totally unlike each other. Oliver, the elder, is envious of his younger brother and tries to kill him. Orlando has all the qualities a gentleman should have, despite the fact that his brother has prevented him from being properly educated. Orlando falls in love with Rosalind, but when he meets her in the Forest he does not recognize her in her disguise as Ganymede. There is another brother, Jaques de Boys, but he is not important and does not appear until the end of the play when he brings a message from the court to Duke Senior.

Touchstone   a professional comedian, who accompanies Rosalind and Celia into the Forest. There he offers many comic, and also sensible, comments on the other characters and their doings.

Jaques   a courtier, living in the Forest with Duke Senior. He represents the 'melancholy' man, a type of person common at the end of the sixteenth century, when it was fashionable to appear sensitive and even neurotic. The melancholy man took a cynical view of the world and society. Jaques is a very complex character: Shakespeare makes him criticize society, but also makes the other characters criticize Jaques.

Adam   an old servant of Sir Rowland de Boys. He represents the honesty and loyalty which the modern world (represented by Oliver de Boys) does not value.

Corin   a wise old shepherd; although he is simple, he is by no means foolish.

Silvius   a silly young shepherd, whose only desire in life is to win the love of Phebe.

Phebe   a young shepherdess. She is cruel to Silvius and mocks his poems, until she falls passionately in love with Ganymede (who of course is Rosalind in disguise).

As You Like It : The play

Act 1

Scene 1 Orlando opens the play with a long speech addressed to Adam. It is a clumsy way of giving information to an audience, but the information is essential, not only for understanding the plot. Orlando introduces one of the play's important themes, the nature of a gentleman. As the son of Sir Rowland de Boys, Orlando is a gentleman by birth, but he has been deprived of a gentleman's education by his brother. When Orlando and Oliver confront each other, there is no doubt about which is the true heir to Sir Rowland. Oliver possesses his father's lands, but there is no trace of Sir Rowland's honourable nature in his character. When he slanders Orlando to Charles, the duke's wrestler, and urges Charles to kill him in the wrestling match, Oliver shows how malicious and unnatural he is. At the end of the scene he admits that he has no cause to hate his brother, and then reveals his motive for wanting Orlando to be killed: Orlando has many virtues, and is very popular,

> and indeed so much in the heart of the world, and especially of my own people, who best know him, that I am altogether misprized. (*1*, 1, 163–5)

Shakespeare is very interested in jealousy arising out of such a situation; he studies it again in this play, and in a later play, *King Lear*, he shows how it can bring about a tragic catastrophe.

Another theme is introduced in this scene when Charles tells Oliver that the outlawed Duke Senior and his loyal supporters have gone into the Forest of Arden,

> and fleet the time carelessly, as they did in the golden world. (*1*, 1, 116–17)

The Golden Age (or 'world') was created by Greek and Latin poets. They claimed that it existed many thousands of years ago,

before men lived in cities and were cruel. It was a pastoral existence: people lived in the country, and found their food growing
around them. There was no need to work for a living; no animals
were slaughtered for meat; people spent their time singing, dancing, and writing poetry. Many English writers at the time of
Shakespeare found the pastoral conventions very attractive. Some
poets, such as Sir Philip Sidney, wrote of shepherds whose entire
existence was given to worshipping the shepherdesses whom they
loved: in the play, Silvius is typical of such shepherd-poets. Other
poets, like Edmund Spenser, made their shepherds speak social
criticism, often comparing court or city life, full of envy and
ambition, with the peace and contentment of country life: Duke
Senior, in *Act 2*, Scene 1, utters such conventional remarks.

The first scene of the play, then, starts off one of the two
central actions of the complex plot. It also introduces three themes:
the nature of a gentleman; the envy that is provoked by goodness;
and the 'golden world' of pastoral convention. Each of these topics
will be examined again—perhaps more than once—in the course
of the play.

Scene 2   The second scene introduces new characters and begins the
second main action of the play. When we first see Rosalind, in this
scene, she is unhappy, and we are never allowed to forget this for
very long. Rosalind is usually gay and witty, not because she is
light-hearted and carefree, but because she has courage and can
hide her sorrows. She decides that she will play at falling in love,
and Celia warns her not to fall in love seriously. Later in the play,
we remember this warning.

Rosalind and Celia are both fond of making puns; many
writers at the time of Shakespeare enjoyed this playing with words.
In the English language, a lot of words have more than one meaning, and some words, which have different meanings and different spellings, sound alike (for instance 'pear', 'pair', and 'pare').
A pun is made when someone amuses himself by reacting to one
meaning of a word when the speaker had intended another: for
instance

> **Touchstone**
> Nay, if I keep not my rank—
> **Rosalind**
> Thou losest thy old smell.   (*1*, 2, 100–1)

The word 'rank' can mean both 'position' (which Touchstone
intends), and 'stench' (which Rosalind pretends to understand).

Touchstone takes no part in the action of the play, but he is very valuable for his observations, full of common-sense, on the ridiculous aspects of the other characters. When Le Beau tells Rosalind and Celia that they have 'lost much good sport' (*1*, 2, 94) because they have not seen a wrestling match in which a young man broke three ribs, Touchstone pretends to be glad that he has learned something new:

Thus men may grow wiser every day. It is the first time that ever I heard breaking of ribs was sport for ladies. (*1*, 2, 127–8)

Touchstone is not stupid; he is a professional comedian. For hundreds of years before the time of Shakespeare, the kings of England employed such fools, whose duties were to entertain the monarch at mealtimes, and at any other time when the king wished to be amused. Fools were permitted to speak freely, and to comment on current affairs and prominent personalities. They were the first English satirists. The fool's position had its dangers; if the fool gave offence, he was likely to be whipped (see *1*, 2, 79). The fool wore a distinctive costume of green and yellow, called his 'motley' (see p. 34). Comments made by Jaques (for instance in *Act 2*, Scene 7, line 13) tell us that Touchstone wears this professional dress all the time that he is in the Forest of Arden. Celia's description of Touchstone as 'our whetstone' (*1*, 2, 52) points to another of the fool's functions. By appearing stupid, the fool gave other men a chance to make fun of him and show how witty they could be. He was what we now call a 'stooge'.

When Le Beau comes on to the stage, Celia greets him in French. This was the language used in the English court after the Norman conquest of England in 1066. Some people thought that to be able to speak French was a sign of good education, but there were other people, especially at the time of Shakespeare, who thought it was a ridiculous affectation. Celia makes fun of Le Beau and his formal speech. By calling the wrestling 'sport', and suggesting that the ladies would have liked to see the deaths of three fine young men, Le Beau shows the inhumanity of court life. His callousness contrasts with the tenderness and care that Rosalind and Celia show when they try to dissuade Orlando from fighting.

Rosalind's remarks to Orlando, and about him, reveal how quickly she is falling in love. At the end of the scene Orlando too admits to himself that he is overcome with a new emotion. Both Rosalind and Orlando have demonstrated an ability to use words well and wittily, but at this moment neither of them is able to express these new feelings. Rosalind can only tell Orlando, obliquely,

> you have wrestled well, and overthrown
> More than your enemies.   (*1*, 2, 243-4)

Orlando cannot speak at all until Rosalind has left the stage, and then he is amazed to find himself so tongue-tied:

> What passion hangs these weights upon my tongue?
> I cannot speak to her, yet she urg'd conference. (*1*, 2, 246-7)

After the wrestling match, we should have a good opinion of Orlando's strength. He showed moral courage when he defied his brother, and again when he politely refused to change his mind about fighting Charles. The fight has proved his physical strength. We must remember this when Orlando is love-sick in the Forest, because he is in danger of appearing weakly romantic.

When Le Beau returns to warn Orlando that he must leave the court, he is not the same as the affected courtier that he appeared to be when he first came on to the stage. What he says about Duke Frederick shows that he is aware of danger in the court, and knows he must be cautious about speaking his mind:

> The duke is humorous; what he is indeed
> More suits you to conceive than I to speak of. (*1*, 2, 255-6)

He prepares us for the duke's anger with Rosalind, and renews one of the play's main themes when he tells us that the anger is

> Grounded upon no other argument
> But that the people praise her for her virtues. (*1*, 2, 268-9)

Scene 3   Although Celia and Rosalind are laughing about Rosalind's love for Orlando, they are really very serious about it. Their light-hearted play with words is only superficial, but even this fun disappears when Duke Frederick orders Rosalind to leave his court. Rosalind defends both herself and her father from the duke's accusations of treachery, and Celia comes to the defence of her cousin. We learn from this defence that Rosalind's father was banished many years ago—yet in an earlier scene we were told that the news at court is that 'the old duke is banished by his younger brother the new duke' (*1*, 1, 98). This contradiction is never satisfactorily resolved, and we have to accept that in *As You Like It* there is no real time scale, only 'dramatic time', which can be lengthened or shortened as Shakespeare pleases.

The most powerful motive affecting the duke's action in banishing Rosalind is not a suspicion that she may be a traitor; he has the same reason for hating Rosalind as Oliver has for hating his brother. The duke tells Celia

> Thou art a fool; she robs thee of thy name,
> And thou wilt show more bright and seem more virtuous
> When she is gone.   (*1*, 3, 78–80)

Le Beau told Orlando in the previous scene that Celia was quite unlike her father (*1*, 2, 260), and now Celia can demonstrate the truth of this.

The decision that Rosalind should dress herself 'all points like a man' (*1*, 3, 114) would not come as a surprise to Shakespeare's audience. The boy actors who played the women's parts were always ready to get back into their own clothes. Dramatists welcomed this, and enjoyed writing scenes for boys, who were women in disguise—who were boys in women's costumes!

Act 2

Scene 1

The first Act of the play was an Act of dispersal, bringing to our attention characters who had good reason for being unhappy in the court. This new Act is set in the Forest of Arden (although Scene 2 takes place at court, and Scene 3 outside Oliver's house). The first Scene shows us the 'golden world' of pastoral convention, referred to by Charles in *Act 1*, Scene 1. Duke Senior utters the proper sentiments, claiming to find country life much superior to life in 'the envious court' (2, 1, 4). But his suggestion, 'shall we go and kill us venison' (2, 1, 21), makes us aware that this life is not, as we had first supposed, the pastoral existence imagined by poets; in real life, men must eat meat, and they cannot do this without slaughtering the animals.

Jaques, it seems, finds life in the forest much the same as life in town, and we are told of his philosophizing over the wounded deer. But the account is given to us at second hand, not by Jaques himself. By this means Shakespeare lets us know, through the amusement of the duke and his followers, that we are not to take Jaques seriously. When we examine his ideas, we can see that they are not very original, and not very profound. He is guilty of sentimentality in his reaction to the stag, and the excessive emotion renders the scene almost comical, with Jaques

> weeping and commenting
> Upon the sobbing deer.   (2, 1, 65-6)

Scene 2   In Scene 2 we return to the court, to learn that Rosalind and Celia have been successful in their plan to run away from the court with Touchstone.

Scene 3   Now Adam takes up the theme of the envy that is aroused in one man at the sight of another man's virtues. His statement of this theme is clear and unmistakable:

> Know you not, master, to some kind of men,
> Their graces serve them but as enemies?
> No more do yours: your virtues, gentle master,
> Are sanctified and holy traitors to you.
> O what a world is this, when what is comely
> Envenoms him that bears it!   (2, 3, 10-15)

By using the words 'sanctified' and 'holy', Adam adds a new dimension to the theme, making it spiritual; perhaps we ought to remember that Envy is one of the Seven Deadly Sins.

Adam also, by offering his savings to help Orlando, introduces a new theme into the play, and Orlando is quick to state this theme in language as clear as Adam used:

> O good old man! how well in thee appears
> The constant service of the antique world,
> When service sweat for duty, not for meed!
> Thou art not for the fashion of these times,
> Where none will sweat but for promotion,
> And having that, do choke their service up
> Even with the having.   (2, 3, 56-62)

Adam is not really a 'character' at all; he is too symbolic to be life-like. His name immediately suggests the Adam of the Bible, and this suggestion is reinforced by Adam's speeches, which are full of biblical phrases and allusions (2, 3, 43-4, for instance). He is a device which Shakespeare uses to expound certain themes; and he is also necessary to bring out Orlando's tenderness and sense of responsibility later in this Act.

Scene 4   Now Shakespeare begins his exploration of the two sides, male and female, of Rosalind's character. In public, and in all outward appearances, she is masculine—able to take responsibility and to carry the burdens of weaker people, brave and cheerful. Privately, and inside the doublet and hose, she is feminine— needing herself the support that she must give to Celia. Some dramatists contemporary with Shakespeare (such as John Fletcher) disguise their female characters as boys, and then appear to forget that they were first intended to be women. Shakespeare never forgets. Here in *As You Like It* Rosalind's disguise is not only a source of comedy (as we shall see in Act 3), but a means by which Shakespeare can present the richness and complexity of Rosalind's character. Conventions of social behaviour in Shakespeare's time (and perhaps even today) forbade a woman to behave naturally— as an equal—in the company of men. Wit and intelligence were not considered desirable in a lady. As Ganymede, Rosalind is free from social restraint: a theatrical convention of disguise releases her from society's conventions of behaviour

The fifteen lines of naturalistic prose conversation at the beginning of *Act 2*, Scene 4 are followed by an episode of very formal verse, spoken by the least life-like of all the characters, Silvius. Silvius is taken from literature, not from life. He is typical of the shepherds in romantic pastoral poetry, who live only to love. For an instant, Rosalind joins in Silvius's poetic dream of love:

> Alas, poor shepherd! Searching of thy wound,
> I have by hard adventure found my own.   (2, 4, 41–2)

His patterned verse and her rhyming couplet are both artificial, remote from everyday speech, and we are made aware that there is something comical about this love when Touchstone joins in with a prose account of his own ludicrous love for Jane Smile.

A number of themes have been introduced in the first part of the play, but this scene brings the most important theme, love, which we are to contemplate in various aspects throughout the rest of the play.

Scene 5   A break in the action, similar to the 'interval' in the theatre today, is given by Amiens' song in *Act 2*, Scene 5. The scene is also useful as an introduction to Jaques. We heard about him in *Act 2*, Scene 1; and in *Act 2*, Scene 7 he will be called upon to perform a serious function. Here he is relaxed, as if he were 'off-duty'.

Scene 6   Since we saw the lords preparing food for the duke in *Act 2, Scene 5*, we are not alarmed in *Act 2, Scene 6* by the condition of Adam when he and Orlando appear in the Forest. This scene shows us another aspect of Orlando, as he tries to cheer and comfort his old servant.

Scene 7   The intellectual discussion between Jaques and Duke Senior on the nature of the satirist and his role in society is one that has no solution: the subject is always topical. It is a matter of opinion, endlessly debatable, whether the satirist should be personally free from reproach, and whether his attack should be directed at a general vice (such as pride) or at an individual instance (one particular proud person).

When Orlando rushes on to the stage, with his sword drawn, the argument stops. Duke Senior reproves Orlando for his unmannerly behaviour, and the mood of the play changes. Once again, in the conversation between Orlando and the duke, court and country life are compared, but this time it is to the advantage of court life. Orlando is proud to say that he is

> inland bred,
> And know some nurture.   (2, 7, 96–7)

Now it seems that the duke is not so happy as he claimed to be in *Act 2, Scene 1*; he admits that he and his followers 'have seen better days' (2, 7, 120). Amiens' song tries to re-assert the superiority of country life:

> Blow, blow, thou winter wind,
> Thou art not so unkind
>   As man's ingratitude.   (2, 7, 174–6)

But the pastoral ideal of the poets has been questioned.

Act 3

Scene 1   It is odd to hear Duke Frederick, in this short scene, rebuke Oliver for his lack of brotherly affection; this is precisely Duke Frederick's fault. The function of this scene becomes apparent at the end of the play, when Oliver has entered the Forest, and Duke Frederick returns the title to his brother. Shakespeare cared little for surprises and last-minute revelations in his play, and always prepares his audience for what is to happen later.

Scene 2   The comedy is now at its height. Corin and Touchstone resume the debate on the relative merits of court life and country life. Touchstone is more obviously clever in his debating techniques, but Corin is not much inferior. Orlando's brief appearance, at the beginning of the scene, as the poetic lover, obsessed with his mistress's beauty, prepares us for the comedy when Rosalind and Celia read aloud the poems he has hung upon the trees. They are very bad poems, as Touchstone remarks. More comedy arises out of Celia's description of her meeting with Orlando, and Rosalind's reactions to the news. Rosalind once again draws attention to her femininity:

> Dost thou think though I am caparisoned like a man, I have
> a doublet and hose in my disposition?   (3, 2, 191-2)

When it is time for her to speak to Orlando, she can quickly adopt a boyish impertinence and 'speak to him like a saucy lackey' (3, 2, 290). She draws a picture in words (but see p. 55) of the conventional poetic lover (3, 2, 362-73), and also of the changeable woman in love (396-407). However, at the end of the scene her anxiety that Orlando 'would but call me Rosalind' (3, 2, 412) betrays how deeply she is affected by him.

Scene 3   Another aspect of love is seen when Touchstone attempts to marry Audrey in the Forest. This is comedy of another sort, the very opposite of Orlando's idealistic emotion. Audrey has never heard the word 'poetical' before, and Touchstone wants to be married in this improper fashion so that,

> not being well married, it will be a good excuse for me
> hereafter to leave my wife.   (3, 3, 83-4)

Scene 4   Alone with Celia, Rosalind does not pretend to be Ganymede; she is a woman, and in love. Celia teases her, and makes fun of Orlando; real love, like Rosalind's, is not afraid of being laughed at.

Scene 5   The love that is now depicted cannot bear laughter. Silvius is the type of lover found only in poetry, who is wholly devoted to his mistress, no matter how cruel she is. Phebe is probably reading a poem he has written when she says 'Thou tell'st me' (3, 5, 10). It was very common for such lover-poets to speak of the killing glances that came from the lady's cruel eyes. Phebe examines the metaphor (called a 'conceit') and shows how ridiculous it is when taken literally. In doing this, however, she is not showing common sense but behaving like another conventional poetic figure, the cruel mistress. Rosalind's speech (*3*, *5*, 35–64) makes this clear, and it is fitting punishment for Phebe that she should herself fall in love with Ganymede, who will never return her love.

Act 4

Scene 1   The comedy increases in Act 4 when Orlando, playing the part of a romantic lover, pleads with Rosalind; she, as Ganymede, adopts an amusingly cynical attitude to love. Suddenly the tone becomes serious, when Rosalind decides that they will 'play' at getting married. This is not all game, and Celia is unwilling to join in—'I cannot say the words' (*4*, 1, 118). A court of law, in Elizabethan England, would accept this ceremony as a binding contract, committing the lovers to each other, although not permitting them to consummate their union without the blessing of the church. The solemn moment soon passes, and Orlando is not aware of it; but when the teasing and laughter are over, and Orlando has left the stage, Rosalind speaks of her love, with few words and much feeling:

> O coz, coz, coz, my pretty little coz, that thou didst know
> how many fathom deep I am in love!   (*4*, 1, 192–3)

Scene 2   Time passes, with a song; and the comedy is renewed for a moment when Silvius brings a letter to Rosalind from Phebe—
Scene 3   a letter in which Phebe makes use of the same poetic devices that she had scorned in *Act 3*, Scene 5. It is a mark of Silvius's love for Phebe that he is willing to carry a letter to his rival, but Rosalind despises him, because love has turned him into a 'tame snake' (*4*, 3, 70).

A more serious note is introduced by Oliver, telling of his rescue from death by Orlando. The episode shows Orlando's courage and, even more important, his generosity. He had an opportunity to repay his brother for Oliver's unnatural hatred of him,

> But kindness, nobler ever than revenge,
> And nature, stronger than his just occasion,
> Made him give battle to the lioness.   (4, 3, 128–30)

Rosalind's reaction to Oliver's speech once again forces us to think of the contrast between her outward appearance as Ganymede, and her real nature. Oliver does not suspect the truth, but the audience can enjoy the irony in the words to cheer 'Ganymede':

> Be of good cheer, youth. You a man! You lack a man's heart.
> (4, 3, 164)

Act 5

Scene 1   When Touchstone finds the country lad, William, it is inevitable that he should make fun of him:

> we that have good wits have much to answer for: we shall be flouting; we cannot hold.   (5, 1, 11–12)

This scene is necessary, not for anything that it tells us about the plot, themes, or characters, but to make a natural break between *Act 4*, Scene 3, and the meeting of Rosalind and Orlando. Also, Robert Armin (and the actors who have played the part of Touchstone after him) would enjoy this opportunity to show their wit.

Scene 2   Now it is time for all the lovers to be collected together: the first Act of this play was an Act of dispersal, and it is balanced here by an Act of union. With a little surprise, we find that Oliver has joined the band of lovers, because he and Celia, on very short acquaintance, have developed a mutual passion. When Rosalind sees Orlando, for the first time after the fight with the lioness, she tries to laugh at her feelings, and Orlando replies to her with the 'conceit' that has been ridiculed so much in this play:

> **Rosalind**
> O my dear Orlando, how it grieves me to see thee wear thy heart in a scarf.
> **Orlando**
> It is my arm.
> **Rosalind**
> I thought thy heart had been wounded with the claws of a lion.
> **Orlando**
> Wounded it is, but with the eyes of a lady.   (5, 2, 19–24)

Now the conceit does not seem absurd; there is so much true feeling in Rosalind's relationship with Orlando that it is a relief for both of them to hide behind a conventional form of speech. Silvius speaks for all the lovers when he begins a definition of love; the others join in the chorus.

Scene 3 Touchstone and Audrey were absent from this meeting, but they have heard of the wedding-day, and Touchstone tells Audrey

> To-morrow is the joyful day, Audrey. To-morrow will we be married.   (5, 3, 1)

Once more, a song marks the passage of time.

Scene 4 The final scene of *As You Like It* evokes a mixture of laughter and tears—tears of happiness. After a ritual repetition of the lovers' promises, Touchstone holds the stage, keeping the audience, as well as the other characters, amused while Rosalind changes out of her doublet and hose, with Celia's help. When the two girls return to the stage, they are accompanied by Hymen, the classical god of marriage. There have been many references to the Greek and Roman gods throughout the play, so it is appropriate for Hymen to appear now.

When the play is performed, the director must decide whether one of the play's characters (such as Amiens, who is not needed in this scene) should impersonate the god, or whether a completely new actor should take this part. If the director chooses the second alternative, he is bringing an element of mystery and magic to the play. There is, certainly, a magical atmosphere in the Forest of Arden: good people have found their happiness within its bounds, and one bad character, Oliver, has been converted from his former nature. In *Act 4*, Scene 3, Rosalind asked if he was the man who had tried to kill Orlando, and she received the answer

> 'Twas I; but 'tis not I. I do not shame
> To tell you what I was, since my conversion
> So sweetly tastes, being the thing I am.   (4, 3, 135-7)

With the arrival of Jaques de Boys, we hear what has happened to the other wicked character, the usurping Duke Frederick:

> to the skirts of this wild wood he came,
> Where, meeting with an old religious man,
> After some question with him, was converted
> Both from his enterprise and from the world.

>   (5, 4, 157-60)

The 'old religious man' belongs to no identifiable religion. The characters in *As You Like It* refer to classical gods *and* use phrases taken from the Bible. The play's action belongs to no particular period, before or after Christ. And the Forest of Arden, despite its English name, is not in England: palm-trees (*3*, 2, 173) and lionesses (*4*, 3, 114) are not found there. Neither time nor place is important in this play: Shakespeare does not make any special effort to be realistic, for mere verisimilitude is inferior to the truth of *As You Like It*. The play presents life not as it is, but as we would like it to be.

The achievement of the play, as we look back from Rosalind's Epilogue, is not simply its creation of an ideal world where the good characters are promised that they will 'live happily ever after', and where bad characters repent of their wickedness and reform their lives. This is what the plot achieves, but *As You Like It* is greater than its plot. The plot provided Shakespeare with a framework, inside which he could arrange themes, points of view, and contrasting attitudes. The final triumph of the play is to have reconciled so many different aspects, so that none dominates at the expense of the others. The various interests, like themes in music, occur and recur through the five Acts, until at the end they, like the characters, have achieved some form of unity within the play's structure and 'Atone together' (*5*, 4, 108).

God buy you, an you talk in blank verse

Jaques' satiric comment on Orlando, the romantic young lover, makes us alert to the changes, in *As You Like It*, from prose to verse, and back again. It is usual, in the drama of this period, for the writers to observe a fairly strict rule dividing characters into those who speak verse and those who speak prose. Verse speakers are kings and queens, lords and ladies, and lovers; prose is spoken by comic characters, servants, and country folk. But Shakespeare does not keep to this division in *As You Like It*. In this play it is, broadly speaking, the topic being discussed that decides whether prose or verse should be the medium of discussion: serious matters are spoken of in verse, and prose is used for mundane affairs. For instance — Duke Frederick banishes Rosalind in verse (*Act 1*, Scene 3), but he watched the wrestling in prose (*Act 1*, Scene 2). When Orlando is explaining his birth and education in the first scene of the play, he speaks in prose; praising Adam's loyalty and industry, his speeches are in verse; comforting his exhausted servant, he returns to prose; and when he appears as the lover of Rosalind, his words naturally fall into the iambic pentameter that Jaques scorns:

> Nay then, God buy you, an you talk in blank verse.
>
> (*4*, 1, 29)

There is nothing artificial about the line that provokes Jaques' ridicule. The words are common, in everyday use, and they are in their normal order. Without Jaques' comment, we might well not notice that here is a perfect blank verse line:

> Good dáy and háppinéss, dear Rósalínd.   (*4*, 1, 28)

Blank verse is ideal for English drama because its rhythms are close to those of normal speech; it is capable of infinite variation, yet at the same time it can impose a pattern on the shapelessness of ordinary speech. Basically, the lines, which are unrhymed, are ten syllables long. The syllables have alternating stresses, just like normal English speech; and they divide into five 'feet'.

Shakespeare uses other verse forms in *As You Like It*. When Silvius is telling Corin about the nature of true love (as he sees it) he speaks a short poem, marked off from its context by repeating two blank verse lines, then half a line:

> If thou remember'st not the slightest folly
> That ever love did make thee run into,
> Thou hast not lov'd   (*2, 4,* 31–3)

Whenever this happens, Shakespeare is paying special attention to the *way* in which a character says something, and the reason is usually obvious: the lines quoted here, for instance, show how poetic and unrealistic the passion is.

Although it is the subject matter that usually determines the form, it is possible to make a few comments on the individual characters, judged in terms of their preference for prose or verse. Touchstone speaks nothing but prose, and this is appropriate for his practical common sense and the mocking nature of his comedy: the prose expresses these qualities, and underlines them. In the same way, Silvius and Phebe, who speak only verse, are defined by their mode of expression. Jaques speaks both prose and verse. The subjects he talks about often demand the dignity of verse, but the character is himself not poetic, as we see from his comment on Orlando's blank verse.

A character like Jaques is valuable to Shakespeare when he wants to alter the tone of an episode. In *Act 2*, Scene 7, for instance, Orlando breaks in on Duke Senior's banquet and demands food for Adam. His entry is highly dramatic—almost melodramatic:

> But forbear, I say,
> He dies that touches any of this fruit,
> Till I and my affairs are answered.   (*1,* 7, 97–9)

Jaques reacts to this emotional outburst with calm reason expressed in prose—and the change from verse to prose makes the request for reason doubly effective:

> An you will not be answered with reason, I must die.
>   (*2,* 7, 100)

The break allows Orlando to change his own tone, modulating through the simple line—'I almost die for food; and let me have it' (*2,* 7, 104)—to the evocation of a ceremonious past:

> If ever you have look'd on better days,
> If ever been where bells have knoll'd to church,

> If ever sat at any good man's feast,
> If ever from your eyelids wip'd a tear,
> And know what 'tis to pity and be pitied.   (*2, 7,* 113–17).

When Duke Senior repeats these words, they become almost ritualistic.

Rosalind speaks most naturally in prose, and everything she says sounds fresh and spontaneous. Her sensible, witty prose makes a sharp contrast to Orlando's feeble verses in *Act 3*, Scene 2, but she can also use prose for her most heart-felt confession of love:

> O coz, coz, coz, my pretty little coz, that thou didst know
> how many fathom deep I am in love.   (*4, 1,* 192–3)

Prose can support Rosalind's many puns, allowing her to show humour and intelligence; the verbal play, depending on double meanings, reflects the appearance of Rosalind dressed as Ganymede. It might be said that Rosalind herself is the physical manifestation of her puns.

The total effect of *As You Like It* is of people talking, not actors declaiming. The mood is informal: dukes can speak prose, and shepherds express themselves in verse, because the barriers that divide the social classes in other plays are not to be found in the Forest of Arden.

Characters in the play

Duke Senior	*living in banishment in the Forest of Arden*
Duke Frederick	*his brother, usurper of his kingdom*
Amiens **Jaques**	*lords accompanying Duke Senior*
Le Beau	*a courtier at Duke Frederick's court*
Charles	*Duke Frederick's wrestler*
Oliver **Jaques** **Orlando**	*sons of Sir Rowland de Boys*
Adam	*an old servant of Sir Rowland's*
Dennis	*Oliver's servant*
Touchstone	*the court fool*
Sir Oliver Martext	*a country parson*
Corin	*an old shepherd*
Silvius	*a young shepherd*
William	*a foolish country lad*
Rosalind	*Duke Senior's daughter*
Celia	*Duke Frederick's daughter*
Phebe	*a shepherdess*
Audrey	*a country lass*
Hymen	*god of marriage, represented in a masque*

Lords   Pages   Attendants

Act 1

Act 1   Scene 1
We learn much in this scene—that
Orlando has little money and that his
brother, Oliver, hates him; that Duke
Senior has been banished from the
court, and that many young men have
joined him in exile; and that Duke
Senior's daughter, Rosalind, remains
in the court with her cousin Celia.
Charles the wrestler asks Oliver to
dissuade Orlando from wrestling, but
Oliver slanders his brother and
persuades Charles to kill him.

2   *by will*: in his will.
     poor a thousand: a mere thousand.
3   *charged*: instructed.
3-4 *on his blessing*: as a condition for
receiving his blessing.
4   *breed*: educate.
5   *school*: university.
6   *goldenly*: well, approvingly.
     profit: progress.
8   *unkept*: uneducated.
10   *stalling*: stabling.
11   *fair with*: in good condition
because of.
12   *taught their manage*: schooled
('manage' is a technical term for the
training of riding horses).
13   *riders*: experts in horse-training.
15   *bound*: indebted.
16-18 *Besides . . . from me*. As well as
giving me nothing so generously, the
way of life that he allows me ('his
countenance') seems to take away from
me the qualities which are mine by
birth.
19   *hinds*: farm labourers.
     bars me: deprives me of.
20   *as much as in him lies*: as far as he
is able.
     mines: undermines.
     gentility: noble birth.
28   *shake me up*: taunt me.

Scene 1 *The orchard near Oliver's house*

Enter Orlando *and* Adam

Orlando
As I remember, Adam, it was upon this fashion:
[he] bequeathed me by will but poor a thousand
crowns, and, as thou sayest, charged my brother, on
his blessing, to breed me well: and there begins my
5 sadness. My brother Jaques he keeps at school, and
report speaks goldenly of his profit: for my part, he
keeps me rustically at home, or, to speak more
properly, stays me here at home unkept; for call you
that 'keeping' for a gentleman of my birth, that
10 differs not from the stalling of an ox? His horses are
bred better; for, besides that they are fair with their
feeding, they are taught their manage, and to that
end riders dearly hired: but I, his brother, gain
nothing under him but growth, for the which his
15 animals on his dunghills are as much bound to him
as I. Besides this nothing that he so plentifully gives
me, the something that nature gave me, his
countenance seems to take from me: he lets me
feed with his hinds, bars me the place of a brother,
20 and, as much as in him lies, mines my gentility with
my education. This is it, Adam, that grieves me;
and the spirit of my father, which I think is within
me, begins to mutiny against this servitude. I will
no longer endure it, though yet I know no wise
25 remedy how to avoid it.

Adam
Yonder comes my master, your brother.

Orlando
Go apart, Adam, and thou shalt hear how he will
shake me up.

[Adam *stands apart*

Enter Oliver

Oliver

Now, sir! what make you here?

Orlando

30 Nothing: I am not taught to make anything.

Oliver

What mar you then, sir?

Orlando

Marry, sir, I am helping you to mar that which God made, a poor unworthy brother of yours, with idleness.

Oliver

35 Marry, sir, be better employed, and be naught awhile.

Orlando

Shall I keep your hogs, and eat husks with them? What prodigal portion have I spent, that I should come to such penury?

Oliver

40 Know you where you are, sir?

Orlando

O sir, very well: here in your orchard.

Oliver

Know you before whom, sir?

Orlando

Ay, better than him I am before knows me. I know you are my eldest brother; and, in the gentle
45 condition of blood, you should so know me. The courtesy of nations allows you my better, in that you are the first-born; but the same tradition takes not away my blood, were there twenty brothers betwixt us. I have as much of my father in me as you; albeit,
50 I confess, your coming before me is nearer to his reverence.

Oliver

What, boy!   [*Strikes him*

Orlando

Come, come, elder brother, you are too young in this.   [*Holds him in a wrestler's grip*

Oliver

55 Wilt thou lay hands on me, villain?

29   *what make you*: what are you doing? Orlando replies as though he thinks 'make' means 'construct'.

32   *Marry*: by the Virgin Mary.

37-9   Orlando refers to the Parable of the Prodigal Son (St. Luke's Gospel 15:11). This tells how the prodigal wasted his inheritance ('portion') in riotous living, until he was compelled to look after another man's pigs and eat the same poor food ('husks') that the pigs ate.

44-5   *gentle . . . blood*: appropriate manner for a gentleman and a brother.

46   *courtesy*: custom.
    allows: acknowledges.

48   *blood*: breeding.

50-1   *your . . . reverence*: because you were born before me, you are entitled to more of the respect ('reverence') that was due to our father.

52   *boy*. This is insulting.

53-4   *young in this*: inexperienced in fighting.

56   *villain :* Oliver intended the meaning 'rogue', but Orlando reacts to the meaning 'peasant'.

61   *railed on thyself :* slandered yourself (by saying that his father could beget a villain).

63   *at accord :* at peace.

69   *qualities :* accomplishments.

71   *exercises :* pursuits.
      may become : may be suited to.
72   *allottery :* share of the inheritance.
73   *testament :* will.

76   *will :* wishes, *and* share of our father's will.

Orlando

I am no villain; I am the youngest son of Sir Rowland de Boys; he was my father, and he is thrice a villain that says such a father begot villains. Wert thou not my brother, I would not take this
60 hand from thy throat till this other had pulled out thy tongue for saying so : thou hast railed on thyself.

Adam

[*Coming forward*] Sweet masters, be patient : for your father's remembrance, be at accord.

Oliver

Let me go, I say.

Orlando

65 I will not, till I please : you shall hear me. My father charged you in his will to give me good education : you have trained me like a peasant, obscuring and hiding from me all gentleman-like qualities. The spirit of my father grows strong in
70 me, and I will no longer endure it ; therefore allow me such exercises as may become a gentleman, or give me the poor allottery my father left me by testament; with that I will go buy my fortunes.

Oliver

And what wilt thou do ? beg, when that is spent ?
75 Well, sir, get you in : I will not long be troubled with you; you shall have some part of your will. I pray you, leave me.

Orlando

I will no further offend you than becomes me for my good.

Oliver

80 Get you with him, you old dog.

Adam

Is 'old dog' my reward ? Most true, I have lost my teeth in your service. God be with my old master! he would not have spoke such a word.

[*Exeunt* Orlando *and* Adam

84   *grow upon me :* grow up and
become a nuisance to me.
85   *physic :* give you medicine.
rankness : excessive growth.

Oliver

Is it even so? begin you to grow upon me? I will
85 physic your rankness, and yet give no thousand
crowns neither. Holla, Dennis!

Enter Dennis

Dennis

Calls your worship?

Oliver

Was not Charles, the duke's wrestler, here to speak
with me?

Dennis

90 So please you, he is here at the door, and importunes access to you.

Oliver

Call him in. [*Exit* Dennis] 'Twill be a good way;
and to-morrow the wrestling is.

Enter Charles

Charles

Good morrow to your worship.

Oliver

95 Good Monsieur Charles, what's the new news at
the new court?

Charles

There's no news at the court, sir, but the old news:
that is, the old duke is banished by his younger
brother the new duke; and three or four loving
100 lords have put themselves into voluntary exile with
him, whose lands and revenues enrich the new
duke; therefore he gives them good leave to wander.

Oliver

Can you tell if Rosalind, the duke's daughter, be
banished with her father?

Charles

105 O, no; for the duke's daughter, her cousin, so loves
her—being ever from their cradles bred together—
that she would have followed her exile, or have
died to stay behind her. She is at the court, and no
less beloved of her uncle than his own daughter;
110 and never two ladies loved as they do.

90   *So please you :* if it pleases you.
90-1 *importunes access to you :* insists
upon coming to see you.

102   *gives . . . wander :* gladly gives
them permission to go where they like.

106   *bred :* brought up.

108   *to stay :* if she were forced to stay.

113 *a many* : a lot of.
114 *Robin Hood*. A romantic character of English folk-lore. He was an outlaw who lived in Sherwood Forest, where he robbed the rich to give their wealth to the poor.
116 *fleet . . . carelessly* : pass the time quickly, free from care.
116-17 *golden world*: Golden Age; see Introduction, p. xi.

121 *disposition* : inclination.
122 *a fall* : a bout of wrestling.
123 *for my credit* : to defend my reputation.

126 *for your love* : because of the love I have for you.
loath to : unwilling to.
foil : overthrow.
129 *withal* : with it.
129-30 *stay . . . intendment* : stop him from carrying out his intentions.
130 *brook* : endure.

134 *kindly* : appropriately.
requite : repay.
136 *underhand* : secret.

139 *emulator* : rival.
140 *contriver* : plotter.
141-2 *I had as lief* : I would rather.

143 *look to't* : be careful.
144 *grace* : honour.
145 *practise . . . poison* : plot to kill you with poison.

Oliver
Where will the old duke live?
Charles
They say he is already in the forest of Arden, and a many merry men with him; and there they live like the old Robin Hood of England. They say
115 many young gentlemen flock to him every day, and fleet the time carelessly, as they did in the golden world.
Oliver
What, you wrestle to-morrow before the new duke?
Charles
Marry, do I, sir; and I came to acquaint you with
120 a matter. I am given, sir, secretly to understand that your younger brother Orlando hath a disposition to come in disguised against me to try a fall. To-morrow, sir, I wrestle for my credit, and he that escapes me without some broken limb shall acquit
125 him well. Your brother is but young and tender; and, for your love, I would be loath to foil him as I must, for my own honour, if he come in: there-fore, out of my love to you, I came hither to acquaint you withal, that either you might stay him from his
130 intendment, or brook such disgrace well as he shall run into, in that it is a thing of his own search and altogether against my will.
Oliver
Charles, I thank thee for thy love to me, which thou shalt find I will most kindly requite. I had myself
135 notice of my brother's purpose herein, and have by underhand means laboured to dissuade him from it, but he is resolute. I'll tell thee, Charles, it is the stubbornest young fellow of France; full of ambi-tion, an envious emulator of every man's good parts,
140 a secret and villainous contriver against me his natural brother: therefore use thy discretion. I had as lief thou didst break his neck as his finger. And thou wert best look to't; for if thou dost him any slight disgrace, or if he do not mightily grace him-
145 self on thee, he will practise against thee by poison, entrap thee by some treacherous device, and never

150   *brotherly* : as a brother, i.e. not objectively.
151   *anatomize* : explain in every detail (the word is used particularly to refer to the dissecting of corpses).

155   *his payment* : what he deserves.
155-6   *go alone* : walk unaided (without crutches).

158-9   *stir this gamester* : provoke this fighter; Oliver speaks scornfully of his brother.

162   *noble device* : honourable intentions.
162-3   *of . . . beloved* : loved by all kinds of people as though he had cast a spell over (enchanted) them.
165   *misprized* : despised.
166   *clear all* : remove all problems.
167   *kindle . . . thither* : encourage the boy to take part in the wrestling.

Act 1   Scene 2
Celia tries to cheer up Rosalind, who is sad because her father is banished. The two girls have fun with Touchstone, and then Le Beau tells them about the wrestling. Duke Frederick's party comes to see more fighting, but the duke is reluctant to see Orlando injured. He wants the girls to dissuade Orlando from fighting, but they are unsuccessful. However, Orlando defeats the professional wrestler.
1   *coz* : cousin.
2-3   *I show . . . of* : I appear merrier than I really am.
5   *learn* : teach.

leave thee till he hath ta'en thy life by some indirect
means or other; for, I assure thee—and almost with
tears I speak it—there is not one so young and so
150   villainous this day living. I speak but brotherly of
him; but should I anatomize him to thee as he is,
I must blush and weep, and thou must look pale
and wonder.
      Charles
      I am heartily glad I came hither to you. If he come
155   to-morrow, I'll give him his payment: if ever he go
alone again, I'll never wrestle for prize more; and
so God keep your worship!   [*Exit*
      Oliver
      Farewell, good Charles. Now will I stir this
gamester. I hope I shall see an end of him; for my
160   soul, yet I know not why, hates nothing more than
he. Yet he's gentle, never schooled and yet learned,
full of noble device, of all sorts enchantingly
beloved, and, indeed so much in the heart of the
world, and especially of my own people, who best
165   know him, that I am altogether misprized. But it
shall not be so long; this wrestler shall clear all:
nothing remains but that I kindle the boy thither,
which now I'll go about.   [*Exit*

Scene 2 *A garden in front of the duke's palace*

Enter Rosalind *and* Celia
      Celia
      I pray thee, Rosalind, sweet my coz, be merry.
      Rosalind
      Dear Celia, I show more mirth than I am mistress
of, and would you yet I were merrier? Unless you
could teach me to forget a banished father, you
5   must not learn me how to remember any extra-
ordinary pleasure.
      Celia
      Herein I see thou lovest me not with the full
weight that I love thee. If my uncle, thy banished

10   *so :* provided that.

11   *take :* accept.

13   *righteously tempered :* properly blended.

14   *estate :* fortune.

16–17   *nor none . . . have :* and is not likely to have any more.

19   *perforce :* by force.
      render : return.

25   *Marry :* by the Virgin Mary.
      I prithee : I pray you.
      withal : with it.

26   *in good earnest :* seriously.

27   *with . . . blush :* protected by your innocence (shown in your blushing).

28   *come off :* withdraw.

30   *Fortune.* The goddess Fortune was traditionally represented holding a wheel which she turned to raise men to happiness or drop them into despair. Celia here compares her with a humble housewife and her spinning-wheel.

33   *would :* wish.

34   *blind woman.* Fortune was painted blind, to signify that her gifts were given at random.

36   *scarce :* rarely.

37   *honest :* virtuous.

38   *ill-favouredly :* unattractively.

father, had banished thy uncle, the duke my father,
10 so thou hadst been still with me, I could have taught my love to take thy father for mine: so wouldst thou, if the truth of thy love to me were so righteously tempered as mine is to thee.

Rosalind
Well, I will forget the condition of my estate, to
15 rejoice in yours.

Celia
You know my father hath no child but I, nor none is like to have; and, truly, when he dies, thou shalt be his heir: for what he hath taken away from thy father perforce, I will render thee again in affection;
20 by mine honour, I will; and when I break that oath, let me turn monster. Therefore, my sweet Rose, my dear Rose, be merry.

Rosalind
From henceforth I will, coz, and devise sports. Let me see; what think you of falling in love?

Celia
25 Marry, I prithee, do, to make sport withal: but love no man in good earnest; nor no further in sport neither, than with safety of a pure blush thou mayst in honour come off again.

Rosalind
What shall be our sport then?

Celia
30 Let us sit and mock the good housewife Fortune from her wheel, that her gifts may henceforth be bestowed equally.

Rosalind
I would we could do so, for her benefits are mightily misplaced, and the bountiful blind woman
35 doth most mistake in her gifts to women.

Celia
'Tis true; for those that she makes fair she scarce makes honest, and those that she makes honest she makes very ill-favouredly.

40-1   *Fortune . . . Nature.* Fortune is
        responsible for acquired gifts (such as
        wealth), but not for natural qualities
        (such as beauty and virtue).

42-3   When Nature has made a beauti-
        ful woman, may she not, by accident,
        fall into the fire (*or be damned in
        hell-fire*)?
44   *flout :* mock.

47   *natural :* fool. Rosalind is making
        fun of Touchstone, because he is not a
        simple fool (a 'natural'), but a
        professional comedian.
49   *Peradventure :* perhaps.

51-2   *hath . . . whetstone :* has sent this
        fool for us to sharpen our wits on.

62   *naught :* rubbish.
        stand to it : swear.

64   *was . . . forsworn :* the knight had
        not broken his oath.

Rosalind

40 Nay, now thou goest from Fortune's office to
Nature's: Fortune reigns in gifts of the world, not
in the lineaments of Nature.

Enter Touchstone

Celia

No? when Nature hath made a fair creature, may
she not by Fortune fall into the fire? Though Nature
hath given us wit to flout at Fortune, hath not

45 Fortune sent in this fool to cut off the argument?

Rosalind

Indeed, there is Fortune too hard for Nature,
when Fortune makes Nature's natural the cutter-
off of Nature's wit.

Celia

Peradventure this is not Fortune's work neither,

50 but Nature's; who, perceiving our natural wits too
dull to reason of such goddesses, hath sent this
natural for our whetstone: for always the dullness
of the fool is the whetstone of the wits. How now,
wit! whither wander you?

Touchstone

55 Mistress, you must come away to your father.

Celia

Were you made the messenger?

Touchstone

No, by mine honour; but I was bid to come for
you.

Rosalind

Where learned you that oath, fool?

Touchstone

60 Of a certain knight that swore by his honour they
were good pancakes, and swore by his honour the
mustard was naught: now, I'll stand to it, the pancakes were naught and the mustard was good, and
yet was not the knight forsworn.

Celia

65 How prove you that, in the great heap of your
knowledge?

Rosalind

Ay, marry, now unmuzzle your wisdom.

Touchstone

Stand you both forth now: stroke your chins, and
swear by your beards that I am a knave.

Celia

70 By our beards—if we had them—thou art.

Touchstone

By my knavery—if I had it—then I were; but if
you swear by that that is not, you are not forsworn:
no more was this knight, swearing by his honour,
for he never had any; or if he had, he had sworn it

75 away before ever he saw those pancakes or that
mustard.

Celia

Prithee, who is 't that thou meanest?

Touchstone

One that old Frederick, your father, loves.

Celia

My father's love is enough to honour him enough.

80 Speak no more of him; you'll be whipped for taxation one of these days.

Touchstone

The more pity, that fools may not speak wisely
what wise men do foolishly.

Celia

By my troth, thou sayest true; for since the little

85 wit that fools have was silenced, the little foolery
that wise men have makes a great show. Here comes
Monsieur Le Beau.

Rosalind

With his mouth full of news.

Celia

Which he will put on us, as pigeons feed their

90 young.

Rosalind

Then we shall be news-crammed.

Celia

All the better; we shall be more marketable.

Enter Le Beau

Bon jour, Monsieur Le Beau: what's the news?

72   *that that is not :* that which does
not exist (in this case, their beards).

74-5   *sworn it away :* i.e. by breaking oaths.

77   *Prithee :* I pray you.

80   *taxation :* slander.

84   *troth :* faith.

89   *put on us :* force on us.

92   *marketable :* easily sold (because
fatter).

93   *Bon jour :* Good day. Celia addresses
Le Beau in French either because he is
French (as his name suggests), or
(more likely) because French was the
polite language at court.

94   *lost :* missed.

95   *colour :* kind.

98   *Destinies :* the Fates, the three
        Greek goddesses who ruled over the life
        of man.
99   *trowel :* a bricklayer's instrument
        for spreading plaster. Celia approves
        Touchstone's exaggerated imitation of
        Le Beau's formal speech.
100   *rank :* position (as a witty fool).
101   *smell :* Rosalind makes a pun on
        'rank' = stink.

106-7   *yet to do :* still to happen.

111   This opening sounds like the start
        of an old story.
112   *proper :* handsome.
113   *presence :* appearance.

114   *bills :* notices.
115   *these presents :* these present
        writings. These are the words on a
        legal document ('bill'), suggested to
        Rosalind by the pun on 'presence'.
117   *which Charles :* the same Charles.

Le Beau
Fair princess, you have lost much good sport.
Celia
95 Sport! Of what colour?
Le Beau
What colour, madam! How shall I answer you?
Rosalind
As wit and fortune will.
Touchstone
Or as the Destinies decree.
Celia
Well said: that was laid on with a trowel.
Touchstone
100 Nay, if I keep not my rank—
Rosalind
Thou losest thy old smell.
Le Beau
You amaze me, ladies: I would have told you of
good wrestling, which you have lost the sight of.
Rosalind
Yet tell us the manner of the wrestling.
Le Beau
105 I will tell you the beginning; and, if it please your
ladyships, you may see the end, for the best is yet
to do; and here, where you are, they are coming to
perform it.
Celia
Well, the beginning, that is dead and buried.
Le Beau
110 There comes an old man and his three sons—
Celia
I could match this beginning with an old tale.
Le Beau
Three proper young men, of excellent growth and
presence—
Rosalind
With bills on their necks, 'Be it known unto all men
115 by these presents.'
Le Beau
The eldest of the three wrestled with Charles, the
duke's wrestler; which Charles in a moment threw

121   *dole :* lamentation.

132   *rib-breaking :* Rosalind is making
        an analogy between a man's ribs and
        the strips of wood, also called 'ribs',
        which form the body of a viol or lute
        and which, if cracked, would spoil the
        music.

139sd *Flourish :* fanfare on the trumpets.

141   *his . . . forwardness :* let his own
        recklessness be responsible for his
        danger.

144   *successfully :* like one who could
        win.

him and broke three of his ribs, that there is little
hope of life in him: so he served the second, and so
120 the third. Yonder they lie; the poor old man, their
father, making such pitiful dole over them that all
the beholders take his part with weeping.

Rosalind
Alas!

Touchstone
But what is the sport, monsieur, that the ladies
125 have lost?

Le Beau
Why, this that I speak of.

Touchstone
Thus men may grow wiser every day: it is the
first time that ever I heard breaking of ribs was
sport for ladies.

Celia
130 Or I, I promise thee.

Rosalind
But is there any else longs to see this broken music
in his sides? is there yet another dotes upon rib-
breaking? Shall we see this wrestling, cousin?

Le Beau
You must, if you stay here; for here is the place
135 appointed for the wrestling, and they are ready to
perform it.

Celia
Yonder, sure, they are coming: let us now stay
and see it.

Flourish. Enter Duke Frederick, Lords,
Orlando, Charles, *and* Attendants

Duke Frederick
140 Come on: since the youth will not be entreated,
his own peril on his forwardness.

Rosalind
Is yonder the man?

Le Beau
Even he, madam.

Celia
Alas! he is too young: yet he looks successfully.

147   *liege :* lord.

149   *odds :* difference.
150   *fain :* gladly.
151   *move :* persuade.

159   *general challenger :* i.e. he has issued a challenge to all men in general.

164-6   *if . . . enterprise :* if you could see and judge yourself properly, the fear of your likely fate ('adventure') would warn you to choose a fight where you stood an equal chance.

169-70   *your . . . misprized :* your reputation will not be dishonoured by this.
170   *suit :* plea.
171   *go forward :* continue.

172-4   *I beseech . . . anything :* please, don't think badly of me, although I know I deserve your bad opinion, for denying anything to such ladies.

Duke Frederick

145 How now, daughter and cousin! are you crept hither to see the wrestling?

Rosalind

Ay, my liege, so please you give us leave.

Duke Frederick

You will take little delight in it, I can tell you, there is such odds in the man: in pity of the challenger's

150 youth I would fain dissuade him, but he will not be entreated. Speak to him, ladies; see if you can move him.

Celia

Call him hither, good Monsieur le Beau.

Duke Frederick

Do so: I'll not be by.   [Duke *goes apart*

Le Beau

155 Monsieur the challenger, the princess calls for you.

Orlando

I attend them with all respect and duty.

Rosalind

Young man, have you challenged Charles the wrestler?

Orlando

No, fair princess; he is the general challenger:

160 I come but in, as others do, to try with him the strength of my youth.

Celia

Young gentleman, your spirits are too bold for your years. You have seen cruel proof of this man's strength: if you saw yourself with your eyes or

165 knew yourself with your judgment, the fear of your adventure would counsel you to a more equal enterprise. We pray you, for your own sake, to embrace your own safety and give over this attempt.

Rosalind

Do, young sir: your reputation shall not therefore

170 be misprized. We will make it our suit to the duke that the wrestling might not go forward.

Orlando

I beseech you, punish me not with your hard thoughts, wherein I confess me much guilty, to

176 *foiled* : overthrown.
177 *gracious* : graced by Fortune.

181 *supplied* : occupied.

183 *would* : wish.

185 *eke out* : support.

186 *deceived* : i.e. by having under-
estimated him as a wrestler.

191 *working* : ambition.

193 *warrant* : assure.

198 *Hercules* : the Roman hero famed for
his strength.
be thy speed : assist you.

deny so fair and excellent ladies anything. But let
175 your fair eyes and gentle wishes go with me to my
trial: wherein if I be foiled, there is but one shamed
that was never gracious; if killed, but one dead that
is willing to be so. I shall do my friends no wrong,
for I have none to lament me; the world no injury,
180 for in it I have nothing; only in the world I fill up
a place, which may be better supplied when I have
made it empty.
Rosalind
The little strength that I have, I would it were
with you.
Celia
185 And mine, to eke out hers.
Rosalind
Fare you well. Pray heaven I be deceived in you!
Celia
Your heart's desires be with you!
Charles
Come, where is this young gallant that is so
desirous to lie with his mother earth?
Orlando
190 Ready, sir; but his will hath in it a more modest
working.
Duke Frederick
You shall try but one fall.
Charles
No, I warrant your Grace, you shall not entreat
him to a second, that have so mightily persuaded
195 him from a first.
Orlando
You mean to mock me after; you should not have
mocked me before: but come your ways.
Rosalind
Now Hercules be thy speed, young man!
Celia
I would I were invisible, to catch the strong fellow
200 by the leg.   [*Charles and* Orlando *wrestle*
Rosalind
O excellent young man!
Celia
If I had a thunderbolt in mine eye, I can tell who
should down.   [*Charles is thrown. Shout*

Duke Frederick
No more, no more.
Orlando
205 Yes, I beseech your Grace: I am not yet well
breathed.
Duke Frederick
How dost thou, Charles?
Le Beau
He cannot speak, my lord.
Duke Frederick
Bear him away. What is thy name, young man?
[*Charles* is carried out
Orlando
210 Orlando, my liege; the youngest son of Sir Rowland
de Boys.
Duke Frederick
I would thou hadst been son to some man else:
The world esteem'd thy father honourable,
But I did find him still mine enemy:
215 Thou shouldst have better pleas'd me with this
deed,
Hadst thou descended from another house.
But fare thee well; thou art a gallant youth:
I would thou hadst told me of another father.
[*Exeunt* Duke Frederick, Attendants,
Touchstone, *and* Le Beau
Celia
220 Were I my father, coz, would I do this?
Orlando
I am more proud to be Sir Rowland's son,
His youngest son; and would not change that
calling,
To be adopted heir to Frederick.
Rosalind
My father lov'd Sir Rowland as his soul,
225 And all the world was of my father's mind.
Had I before known this young man his son,
I should have given him tears unto entreaties,
Ere he should thus have ventur'd.
Celia   Gentle cousin,
Let us go thank him and encourage him:
230 My father's rough and envious disposition
Sticks me at heart. Sir, you have well deserv'd:

205-6 *well breathed :* warmed up.

210 *liege :* lord.

214 *still :* always.

216 *house :* family.

225 *was . . . mind :* shared my father's opinion.

227 *unto :* as well as.

231 *Sticks . . . heart :* is painful to my heart.

If you do keep your promises in love
But justly, as you have exceeded all promise,
Your mistress shall be happy.
  Rosalind   Gentleman,
     [*Giving him a necklace*
235 Wear this for me, one out of suits with fortune,
That could give more, but that her hand lacks
  means.
Shall we go, coz?
  Celia Ay. Fare you well, fair gentleman.
  Orlando
Can I not say, 'I thank you'? My better parts
Are all thrown down, and that which here stands up
240 Is but a quintain, a mere lifeless block.
  Rosalind
He calls us back: my pride fell with my fortunes;
I'll ask him what he would. Did you call, sir?
Sir, you have wrestled well, and overthrown
More than your enemies.
  Celia   Will you go, coz?
  Rosalind
245 Have with you. Fare you well.
     [*Exeunt* Rosalind *and* Celia
  Orlando
What passion hangs these weights upon my tongue?
I cannot speak to her, yet she urg'd conference.
O poor Orlando, thou art overthrown!
Or Charles or something weaker masters thee.

    Enter Le Beau
  Le Beau
250 Good sir, I do in friendship counsel you
To leave this place. Albeit you have deserv'd
High commendation, true applause and love,
Yet such is now the duke's condition
That he misconsters all that you have done.

---

233 *justly* : exactly.

235 *out of suits* : out of favour.
236 *could give* : would like to give.

240 *quintain* : a dummy which the horseman used to strike with his lance when practising 'tilting'. See illustration, p. 62.
242 *would* : wants.

245 *Have with you* : I'm coming.

247 *urg'd conference* : invited conversation.
249 *Or Charles* : either Charles.

253 *condition* : mood.
254 *misconsters* : misinterprets.

255   *humorous*: moody. Elizabethan medical theory taught that every man was composed of four humours— blood, phlegm, choler, and melancholy—and the proportion of these in the body determined the man's disposition.

255-6   It is better that you should imagine what he is really like than that I should tell you.

264   *whose*: their.

268   *Grounded*: based.
       argument: reason.

271   *on my life*: I'll bet my life on it.

275   *bounden*: indebted.

276   *smother*: thicker smoke; the modern equivalent for Orlando's phrase is 'from the frying-pan into the fire'.

Act 1   Scene 3

Rosalind confesses to Celia that she has fallen in love with Orlando. Duke Frederick banishes Rosalind from his court, but when her father has left the stage, Celia announces that she will accompany Rosalind into banishment. They decide that they will go to find Rosalind's father in the Forest of Arden, and that for safety they ought to disguise themselves.

1   *Cupid*: the classical god of love.

255   The duke is humorous: what he is indeed,
      More suits you to conceive than I to speak of.
         Orlando
      I thank you, sir; and pray you, tell me this;
      Which of the two was daughter of the duke,
      That here was at the wrestling?
         Le Beau
260   Neither his daughter, if we judge by manners:
      But yet, indeed the smaller is his daughter:
      The other is daughter to the banish'd duke,
      And here detain'd by her usurping uncle,
      To keep his daughter company; whose loves
265   Are dearer than the natural bond of sisters.
      But I can tell you that of late this duke
      Hath ta'en displeasure 'gainst his gentle niece,
      Grounded upon no other argument
      But that the people praise her for her virtues,
270   And pity her for her good father's sake;
      And, on my life, his malice 'gainst the lady
      Will suddenly break forth. Sir, fare you well:
      Hereafter, in a better world than this,
      I shall desire more love and knowledge of you.
         Orlando
275   I rest much bounden to you: fare you well.
                                    [*Exit* Le Beau
      Thus must I from the smoke into the smother;
      From tyrant duke unto a tyrant brother.
      But heavenly Rosalind!   [*Exit*

Scene 3 *A room in the palace*

         Enter Celia *and* Rosalind
         Celia
      Why, cousin! why, Rosalind! Cupid have mercy!
      Not a word?
         Rosalind
      Not one to throw at a dog.
         Celia
      No, thy words are too precious to be cast away

8   *mad* : depressed.

11   *my child's father* : i.e. Orlando, the man she would like to marry.
12   *briars* : thorn-bushes (i.e. difficulties).
     working-day : everyday.
13   *burrs* : heads of thistles; when they are thrown in fun ('holiday foolery') the prickles cling to one's clothes.

18   *Hem* : cough. Celia puns on 'bur' = a tickle in the throat.

21   *take the part* : are on the side.

23   *try* : i.e. try a bout of wrestling with Orlando.
23-4 *in . . . fall* : even though you risk falling.
24-5 *turning . . . service* : setting aside these jokes (a servant was said to be turned out of service when he lost his job).
25   *in good earnest* : seriously.
25-6 *on . . . sudden* : so suddenly.

30   *By . . . chase* : according to this logic.

33   *faith* : by my faith.

5 upon curs; throw some of them at me; come, lame me with reasons.

Rosalind
Then there were two cousins laid up; when the one should be lamed with reasons and the other mad without any.

Celia
10 But is all this for your father?

Rosalind
No, some of it is for my child's father: O, how full of briars is this working-day world!

Celia
They are but burrs, cousin, thrown upon thee in holiday foolery: if we walk not in the trodden paths,
15 our very petticoats will catch them.

Rosalind
I could shake them off my coat: these burrs are in my heart.

Celia
Hem them away.

Rosalind
I would try, if I could cry 'hem', and have him.

Celia
20 Come, come; wrestle with thy affections.

Rosalind
O, they take the part of a better wrestler than myself!

Celia
O, a good wish upon you! you will try in time, in despite of a fall. But, turning these jests out of
25 service, let us talk in good earnest: is it possible, on such a sudden, you should fall into so strong a liking with old Sir Rowland's youngest son?

Rosalind
The duke my father loved his father dearly.

Celia
Doth it therefore ensue that you should love his son
30 dearly? By this kind of chase, I should hate him, for my father hated his father dearly; yet I hate not Orlando.

Rosalind
No, faith, hate him not, for my sake.

Celia

35 Why should I not? doth he not deserve well?

Rosalind

Let me love him for that; and do you love him,
because I do. Look, here comes the duke.

Celia

With his eyes full of anger.

Enter Duke Frederick, *with* Lords

Duke Frederick

Mistress, dispatch you with your safest haste,

40 And get you from our court.

Rosalind   Me, uncle?

Duke Frederick   You, cousin:

Within these ten days if that thou be'st found
So near our public court as twenty miles,
Thou diest for it.

Rosalind   I do beseech your Grace.

Let me the knowledge of my fault bear with me.

45 If with myself I hold intelligence,
Or have acquaintance with mine own desires,
If that I do not dream or be not frantic—
As I do trust I am not—then, dear uncle,
Never so much as in a thought unborn

50 Did I offend your highness.

Duke Frederick   Thus do all traitors:

If their purgation did consist in words,
They are as innocent as grace itself:
Let it suffice thee that I trust thee not.

Rosalind

Yet your mistrust cannot make me a traitor:

55 Tell me whereon the likelihood depends.

Duke Frederick

Thou art thy father's daughter; there's enough.

Rosalind

So was I when your highness took his dukedom;
So was I when your highness banish'd him.

39   *dispatch . . . haste :* hurry up, the
     faster you can go, the safer it will be
     for you.

40   *cousin :* kinswoman.

45-6 If I know myself, or understand my
     own thoughts.

47   *frantic :* mad.

51   *purgation :* proof of innocence.

53   *suffice thee :* be enough for you.

55   *whereon :* on what grounds.

60 *friends* : family.
61 *What's that* : what does that matter.
62 *good my liege* : my good lord.
63 *my poverty is treacherous* : that because I am poor I am a traitor.

65 *stay'd* : kept.
66 *with . . . along* : wandered off together with (alongside) her father.

68 *remorse* : pity.

71 *still* : always.
72 *at an instant* : at the same moment.
73 *Juno's swans*. In Greek and Roman mythology, swans drew the chariot of Venus, goddess of love. But swans are royal birds (those on the River Thames are still owned by the Queen), and perhaps this is why Shakespeare made a mistake and gave them to Juno, queen of the gods.
75 *subtle* : cunning.
78 *name* : proper reputation.

81 *doom* : sentence.

87 *greatness* : power.

Treason is not inherited, my lord;
60 Or, if we did derive it from our friends,
What's that to me? my father was no traitor:
Then, good my liege, mistake me not so much
To think my poverty is treacherous.
> **Celia**
Dear sovereign, hear me speak.
> **Duke Frederick**
65 Ay, Celia; we stay'd her for your sake;
Else had she with her father rang'd along.
> **Celia**
I did not then entreat to have her stay:
It was your pleasure and your own remorse.
I was too young that time to value her;
70 But now I know her: if she be a traitor,
Why so am I; we still have slept together,
Rose at an instant, learn'd, play'd, ate together;
And wheresoe'er we went, like Juno's swans,
Still we went coupled and inseparable.
> **Duke Frederick**
75 She is too subtle for thee; and her smoothness,
Her very silence and her patience,
Speak to the people, and they pity her.
Thou art a fool: she robs thee of thy name;
And thou wilt show more bright and seem more virtuous
80 When she is gone. Then open not thy lips:
Firm and irrevocable is my doom
Which I have pass'd upon her; she is banish'd.
> **Celia**
Pronounce that sentence then on me, my liege:
I cannot live out of her company.
> **Duke Frederick**
85 You are a fool. You, niece, provide yourself:
If you outstay the time, upon mine honour,
And in the greatness of my word, you die.
> [*Exeunt* Duke Frederick *and* Lords
> **Celia**
O my poor Rosalind! whither wilt thou go?
Wilt thou change fathers? I will give thee mine.

90   *charge :* order (Celia is not stern, but speaks lovingly as she says this).

92   *Prithee :* I pray you.

96   *sunder'd :* separated.

98   *devise :* plan.

100   Do not try to endure this change of fortune by yourself.

102   *now . . . pale :* now pale in sympathy with our sorrows.

110   *umber :* a brown paint (which would make the white-skinned court ladies look like peasants).
      smirch : stain.
111   *The like do you :* you do the same.
112   *stir :* provoke.
113   *common :* usually.
114   *suit me all points :* dress myself in every way.
115   *curtle-axe :* cutlass (a short sword).

118   *swashing :* swaggering.
      outside : appearance.
119   *mannish cowards :* cowardly men.
120   *outface it :* brazen it out.
      semblances : appearances.

90   I charge thee, be not thou more griev'd than I am.
        Rosalind
      I have more cause.
        Celia   Thou hast not, cousin;
      Prithee, be cheerful; know'st thou not, the duke
      Hath banish'd me, his daughter?
        Rosalind   That he hath not.
        Celia
      No, hath not? Rosalind lacks then the love
95   Which teacheth thee that thou and I am one:
      Shall we be sunder'd? shall we part, sweet girl?
      No: let my father seek another heir.
      Therefore devise with me how we may fly,
      Whither to go, and what to bear with us:
100   And do not seek to take your change upon you,
      To bear your griefs yourself and leave me out;
      For, by this heaven, now at our sorrows pale,
      Say what thou canst, I'll go along with thee.
        Rosalind
      Why, whither shall we go?
        Celia
105   To seek my uncle in the forest of Arden.
        Rosalind
      Alas, what danger will it be to us,
      Maids as we are, to travel forth so far!
      Beauty provoketh thieves sooner than gold.
        Celia
      I'll put myself in poor and mean attire,
110   And with a kind of umber smirch my face;
      The like do you: so shall we pass along
      And never stir assailants.
        Rosalind   Were it not better,
      Because that I am more than common tall,
      That I did suit me all points like a man?
115   A gallant curtle-axe upon my thigh,
      A boar-spear in my hand; and, in my heart
      Lie there what hidden woman's fear there will,
      We'll have a swashing and a martial outside,
      As many other mannish cowards have
120   That do outface it with their semblances.

123 *Ganymede*. Jove (or Jupiter, king of the classical gods) fell in love with a mortal boy and carried him to Mount Olympus to be his cup-bearer. The name is particularly appropriate because Ganymede was an effeminate boy, while the disguised Rosalind will be a woman with a masculine appearance.

126 *Aliena*. This means 'the stranger'.

127 *assay'd*: tried.

131 *woo*: persuade.

Celia
What shall I call thee when thou art a man?
Rosalind
I'll have no worse a name than Jove's own page,
And therefore look you call me Ganymede.
But what will you be call'd?
Celia
125 Something that hath a reference to my state:
No longer Celia, but Aliena.
Rosalind
But, cousin, what if we assay'd to steal
The clownish fool out of your father's court?
Would he not be a comfort to our travel?
Celia
130 He'll go along o'er the wide world with me;
Leave me alone to woo him. Let's away,
And get our jewels and our wealth together,
Devise the fittest time and safest way
To hide us from pursuit that will be made
135 After my flight. Now go we in content
To liberty and not to banishment.   [*Exeunt*

Act 2

Act 2   Scene 1

Duke Senior and the lords who share
his exile take pleasure in their country
life. The duke comments on the
lessons he learns from nature, and one
of the lords tells how Jaques, too,
finds moral teaching in the death of
a stag.

1   *co-mates :* companions.
2   *old custom :* familiarity.
3   *painted pomp :* artificial splendour.
5   *but . . . Adam :* no more than the
    hardships felt by all men since Adam.
6   *as :* such as.

11 *feelingly persuade me :* teach me
    through my senses.

13 *toad.* The Elizabethans believed that
    toads were poisonous, but that they
    had a stone in their heads which could
    act as an antidote to the poison.
15 *exempt from public haunt :* free from
    interruption by all sorts of people.

20 *style :* i.e. of living.

22 *irks me :* distresses me.
    fools : simple creatures.
23 *burghers :* citizens.
24 *confines :* territories.
    forked heads : arrows.

27 *in that kind :* on that subject.

Scene 1 *The Forest of Arden*

Enter Duke Senior, Amiens, *and other*
Lords, *dressed like Foresters*

Duke Senior
Now, my co-mates and brothers in exile,
Hath not old custom made this life more sweet
Than that of painted pomp? Are not these woods
More free from peril than the envious court?
5 Here feel we but the penalty of Adam,
The seasons' difference, as, the icy fang
And churlish chiding of the winter's wind;
Which, when it bites and blows upon my body,
Even till I shrink with cold, I smile and say
10 'This is no flattery: these are counsellors
That feelingly persuade me what I am.'
Sweet are the uses of adversity,
Which like a toad, ugly and venomous,
Wears yet a precious jewel in his head;
15 And this our life, exempt from public haunt,
Finds tongues in trees, books in the running brooks,
Sermons in stones, and good in every thing.
Amiens
I would not change it. Happy is your Grace,
That can translate the stubbornness of fortune
20 Into so quiet and so sweet a style.
Duke Senior
Come, shall we go and kill us venison?
And yet it irks me the poor dappled fools,
Being native burghers of this desert city,
Should, in their own confines, with forked heads
25 Have their round haunches gor'd.
First Lord   Indeed, my lord,
The melancholy Jaques grieves at that;
And, in that kind, swears you do more usurp

30   *along :* alongside.
31   *antique :* ancient.
32   *brawls :* chatters (imitating the
sound of the stream).
33   *the which :* this.
     sequester'd : separated from the
herd.

40   *piteous :* pitiful.
41   *Much marked of :* closely observed
by.

43   *Augmenting :* adding to.

45   *similes :* comparisons.
46   *needless :* i.e. not needing more
water.
47   *testament :* will.
48   *worldlings :* worldly creatures—
i.e. men.
48-9 Giving more to the people who
already have too much.
50   *of :* by.
     velvet friend : velvet-coated family
(it is the stag that has been
abandoned).
51-2 The sight of unhappiness turns
away the stream ('flux') of fellowship.
52   *anon :* presently.
     careless : carefree.
53   *Full of the pasture :* well-fed.
56   *'Tis just the fashion :* that's exactly
how it is.

61   *mere :* no more than.
     and what's worse : and things that
are still worse.
62   *kill them up :* kill them all off.
63   *assign'd :* appointed (by God).

Than doth your brother that hath banish'd you.
To-day my Lord of Amiens and myself
30 Did steal behind him as he lay along
Under an oak whose antique root peeps out
Upon the brook that brawls along this wood;
To the which place a poor sequester'd stag,
That from the hunters' aim had ta'en a hurt,
35 Did come to languish; and, indeed, my lord,
The wretched animal heav'd forth such groans
That their discharge did stretch his leathern coat
Almost to bursting, and the big round tears
Cours'd one another down his innocent nose
40 In piteous chase; and thus the hairy fool,
Much marked of the melancholy Jaques,
Stood on th' extremest verge of the swift brook,
Augmenting it with tears.
    Duke Senior   But what said Jaques?
Did he not moralize this spectacle?
    First Lord
45 O, yes, into a thousand similes.
First, for his weeping into the needless stream;
'Poor deer,' quoth he, 'thou mak'st a testament
As worldlings do, giving thy sum of more
To that which had too much': then, being there
    alone,
50 Left and abandon'd of his velvet friend;
''Tis right,' quoth he; 'thus misery doth part
The flux of company': anon, a careless herd,
Full of the pasture, jumps along by him
And never stays to greet him; 'Ay,' quoth Jaques,
55 'Sweep on, you fat and greasy citizens;
'Tis just the fashion; wherefore do you look
Upon that poor and broken bankrupt there?'
Thus most invectively he pierceth through
The body of the country, city, court,
60 Yea, and of this our life, swearing that we
Are mere usurpers, tyrants, and what's worse,
To fright the animals and to kill them up
In their assign'd and native dwelling-place.
    Duke Senior
And did you leave him in this contemplation?

65 *commenting* : moralizing.

67 *cope* : debate with.
68 *matter* : ideas.

69 *straight* : immediately.

Act 2   Scene 2
Duke Frederick has missed his
daughter, and suspects that Orlando
may have run away with Celia and
Rosalind.

3   Know about this and have allowed
it to happen.

6   *a-bed* : in bed.
7   *untreasur'd* : robbed of its treasure.

8   *roynish* : vulgar.
9   *wont* : accustomed.

13 *parts* : qualities.
14 *foil* : defeat.

17 *gallant* : fine gentleman (he speaks
sarcastically of Orlando).

19 *suddenly* : at once.
20 *inquisition* : inquiry.
    quail : give up.
21 *bring again* : bring back.

Second Lord
65 We did, my lord, weeping and commenting
Upon the sobbing deer.
    Duke Senior   Show me the place.
I love to cope him in these sullen fits,
For then he's full of matter.
    Second Lord
I'll bring you to him straight.   [*Exeunt*

Scene 2 *A room in the palace*

Enter Duke Frederick, Lords, *and*
Attendants
    Duke Frederick
Can it be possible that no man saw them?
It cannot be: some villains of my court
Are of consent and sufferance in this.
    First Lord
I cannot hear of any that did see her.
5   The ladies, her attendants of her chamber,
Saw her a-bed; and, in the morning early,
They found the bed untreasur'd of their mistress.
    Second Lord
My lord, the roynish clown, at whom so oft
Your Grace was wont to laugh, is also missing.
10 Hisperia, the princess' gentlewoman,
Confesses that she secretly o'erheard
Your daughter and her cousin much commend
The parts and graces of the wrestler
That did but lately foil the sinewy Charles;
15 And she believes, wherever they are gone,
That youth is surely in their company.
    Duke Frederick
Send to his brother; fetch that gallant hither;
If he be absent, bring his brother to me;
I'll make him find him. Do this suddenly,
20 And let not search and inquisition quail
To bring again these foolish runaways.   [*Exeunt*

Act 2 Scene 3

Adam tells Orlando that he must not come home because his brother is planning to murder him. He offers his life's savings to his master, and volunteers to accompany him.

3 *memory :* reminder.
4 *what makes you :* what are you doing?

7 *fond :* foolish.
8 *bonny :* strong.
   prizer : prize-fighter.
   humorous : moody (see note to 1, 2, 255).

12 *No more do yours :* your virtues do no more for you (i.e. they are your enemies).
14 *comely :* becoming, praise-worthy.
15 *Envenoms :* poisons.

23 *use to lie :* usually sleep.

25 *cut you off :* kill you.
26 *practices :* plots.
27 *no place :* no place for you, no home.
    butchery : slaughterhouse.

30 *so :* provided that.

Scene 3 *Outside Oliver's house*

Enter Orlando *and* Adam, *meeting*

Orlando
Who's there?
   Adam
What! my young master? O my gentle master!
O my sweet master! O you memory
Of old Sir Rowland! why, what make you here?
5 Why are you virtuous? Why do people love you?
And wherefore are you gentle, strong, and valiant?
Why would you be so fond to overcome
The bonny prizer of the humorous duke?
Your praise is come too swiftly home before you.
10 Know you not, master, to some kind of men
Their graces serve them but as enemies?
No more do yours: your virtues, gentle master,
Are sanctified and holy traitors to you.
O, what a world is this, when what is comely
15 Envenoms him that bears it!
   Orlando
Why, what's the matter?
   Adam   O unhappy youth!
Come not within these doors; within this roof
The enemy of all your graces lives.
Your brother—no, no brother; yet the son—
20 Yet not the son, I will not call him son
Of him I was about to call his father—
Hath heard your praises, and this night he means
To burn the lodging where you use to lie,
And you within it: if he fail of that,
25 He will have other means to cut you off.
I overheard him and his practices.
This is no place; this house is but a butchery:
Abhor it, fear it, do not enter it.
   Orlando
Why, whither, Adam, wouldst thou have me go?
   Adam
30 No matter whither, so you come not here.

32 *boisterous :* unruly, violent.

35 *do how I can :* whatever happens to me.

37 *a diverted blood :* unnatural (a blood relationship that has turned from its natural direction).
bloody : murderous.

39 *thrifty hire I sav'd :* the thrifty savings from my wages.

40 *to be my foster-nurse :* to care for me.

41 When my old limbs are lame and unfit for service.

42 And as an old man I am thrown into a corner and not noticed.

43-4 Adam refers to two passages in the Bible—Psalm 147:9 and St. Matthew's Gospel 10:29.

44 *providently caters for :* with care provides for.

47 *lusty :* healthy.

49 *rebellious :* causing rebellion (disorder) in the body.

50-1 Nor did I shamelessly ('with unbashful forehead') seek ('woo') the things that cause weakness and illness.

57 *constant :* faithful.
antique : ancient.

58 *sweat :* sweated.
meed : reward.

61 *choke their service up :* withdraw their labours.

62 *Even with the having :* as soon as they have what they wanted (i.e. 'promotion').

63 *a rotten tree :* i.e. Orlando himself.

65 *In lieu of :* in return for.
pains : cares.
husbandry : farming.

66 *come thy ways :* come along.
We'll find ('light upon') and settle in some humble way of life that will content us.

Orlando
What! wouldst thou have me go and beg my food?
Or with a base and boisterous sword enforce
A thievish living on the common road?
This I must do, or know not what to do:
35 Yet this I will not do, do how I can;
I rather will subject me to the malice
Of a diverted blood and bloody brother.
Adam
But do not so. I have five hundred crowns,
The thrifty hire I sav'd under your father,
40 Which I did store to be my foster-nurse
When service should in my old limbs lie lame,
And unregarded age in corners thrown.
Take that; and He that doth the ravens feed,
Yea, providently caters for the sparrow,
45 Be comfort to my age! Here is the gold;
All this I give you. Let me be your servant:
Though I look old, yet I am strong and lusty;
For in my youth I never did apply
Hot and rebellious liquors in my blood,
50 Nor did not with unbashful forehead woo
The means of weakness and debility;
Therefore my age is as a lusty winter,
Frosty, but kindly. Let me go with you;
I'll do the service of a younger man
55 In all your business and necessities.
Orlando
O good old man! how well in thee appears
The constant service of the antique world,
When service sweat for duty, not for meed!
Thou art not for the fashion of these times,
60 Where none will sweat but for promotion,
And having that, do choke their service up
Even with the having: it is not so with thee.
But, poor old man, thou prun'st a rotten tree,
That cannot so much as a blossom yield,
65 In lieu of all thy pains and husbandry.
But come thy ways, we'll go along together,
And ere we have thy youthful wages spent,
We'll light upon some settled low content.

Adam

Master, go on, and I will follow thee
70 To the last gasp with truth and loyalty.
From seventeen years till now almost fourscore
Here lived I, but now live here no more.
At seventeen years many their fortunes seek;
But at fourscore it is too late a week:
75 Yet fortune cannot recompense me better
Than to die well and not my master's debtor.

[*Exeunt*

74   *too late a week :* too late in the day.

Act 2   Scene 4
Rosalind and Celia overhear Silvius
telling Corin about his love. They ask
Corin to help them, because they are
tired and hungry.

1   *Jupiter .* king of the classical gods.

6   *weaker vessel :* i.e. the woman;
Shakespeare is quoting the First
Epistle of Peter 3:4.
doublet and hose : jacket and breeches.

Scene 4 *The Forest of Arden*

Enter Rosalind *in boy's clothes,* Celia
dressed like a shepherdess, and Touchstone

Rosalind
O Jupiter! how weary are my spirits.

Touchstone
I care not for my spirits, if my legs were not
weary.

Rosalind
I could find in my heart to disgrace my man's
5 apparel and to cry like a woman; but I must comfort the weaker vessel, as doublet and hose ought
to show itself courageous to petticoat: therefore,
courage, good Aliena.

9   *bear with me :* have patience with me.

Celia

I pray you, bear with me: I cannot go no further.

Touchstone

10 For my part, I had rather bear with you than bear
you; yet I should bear no cross if I did bear you,
for I think you have no money in your purse.

Rosalind

Well, this is the forest of Arden.

Touchstone

Ay, now am I in Arden; the more fool I: when I was
15 at home, I was in a better place: but travellers
must be content.

Rosalind

Ay, be so, good Touchstone. Look you, who comes
here; a young man and an old in solemn talk.

Enter Corin *and* Silvius

Corin

That is the way to make her scorn you still.

Silvius

20 O Corin, that thou knew'st how I do love her!

Corin

I partly guess, for I have lov'd ere now.

Silvius

No, Corin; being old, thou canst not guess,
Though in thy youth thou wast as true a lover
As ever sigh'd upon a midnight pillow:

25 But if thy love were ever like to mine—
As sure I think did never man love so—
How many actions most ridiculous
Hast thou been drawn to by thy fantasy?

Corin

Into a thousand that I have forgotten.

Silvius

30 O thou didst then ne'er love so heartily.
If thou remember'st not the slightest folly
That ever love did make thee run into,
Thou hast not lov'd:
Or if thou hast not sat as I do now,
35 Wearying thy hearer in thy mistress' praise,
Thou hast not lov'd:
Or if thou hast not broke from company
Abruptly, as my passion now makes me,

11 *no cross :* no burden.
12 *no money.* Touchstone's pun refers to
coins which were stamped with a cross.

14 *the more fool I :* I am a bigger fool
now than I was before (when I was at
home).

21 *partly :* to some extent.

23 *Though :* even though.
24 *a midnight pillow :* a pillow at
midnight.
25 *like to :* similar to.

28 *to :* into.
fantasy : affections.

35 *in thy mistress' praise :* by praising
your mistress.

Thou hast not lov'd.

40 O Phebe, Phebe, Phebe!   [*Exit*

Rosalind

Alas, poor shepherd! Searching of thy wound,
I have by hard adventure found mine own.

Touchstone

And I mine. I remember, when I was in love I
broke my sword upon a stone, and bid him take

45 that for coming a-night to Jane Smile; and I
remember the kissing of her batler, and the cow's
dugs that her pretty chapped hands had milked;
and I remember the wooing of a peascod instead
of her, from whom I took two cods, and giving her

50 them again, said with weeping tears, 'Wear these
for my sake.' We that are true lovers run into
strange capers; but as all is mortal in nature, so is
all nature in love mortal in folly.

Rosalind

Thou speakest wiser than thou art ware of.

Touchstone

55 Nay, I shall ne'er be ware of mine own wit till
I break my shins against it.

Rosalind

Jove, Jove! this shepherd's passion
Is much upon my fashion.

Touchstone

And mine; but it grows something stale with me.

Celia

60 I pray you, one of you question yond man,
If he for gold will give us any food:
I faint almost to death.

Touchstone   Holla, you clown!

Rosalind

Peace, fool: he's not thy kinsman.

Corin   Who calls?

Touchstone

Your betters, sir.

Corin   Else are they very wretched.

Rosalind

65 Peace, I say. Good even to you, friend.

Corin

And to you, gentle sir, and to you all.

---

41   *Searching* : probing ('Searching' is the technical term given to the surgical examination of a wound).

42   *hard adventure* : bad luck.

44   *him* : i.e. the stone (which Touchstone pretends is his rival).

45   *a-night* : at night.

46   *batler* : wooden beater used for washing clothes.

47   *dugs* : teats.

48   *peascod* : pea plant.

49   *cods* : pea-pods.

52   *capers* : actions.

52–3 As everything in nature must die, so all who are in love are bound to act foolishly.

54   *ware* : aware; Touchstone replies as though Rosalind means 'beware'.

59   *something* : somewhat.

60   *yond* : yonder.

62   *clown* : country fellow; but Rosalind speaks as though Touchstone means 'fool'.

65   *even* : evening.

67 *that* : either.
68 *entertainment* : hospitality.

70 *oppress'd* : exhausted.
71 *faints for succour* : faints with need for help.

75 Corin looks after the sheep but does not collect their wool, i.e. own them.
76 *churlish* : surly.
77 *recks* : cares.

79 *cote* : cottage.
    bounds of feed : pasture-land.
80 *on sale* : being sold.

82 *what is* : what there is.
83 *in my voice* : as far as I can say.

85 *swain* : lover.
    but erewhile : just a short time ago.

87 *if . . . honesty* : if you can do it honestly.

89 *have to pay* : have what is necessary to pay.
90 *mend* : improve.
91 *waste* : spend.

93 *upon report* : when you hear more of it.

95 *feeder* : shepherd.
96 *right suddenly* : without delay.

Rosalind
I prithee, shepherd, if that love or gold
Can in this desert place buy entertainment,
Bring us where we may rest ourselves and feed.
70 Here's a young maid with travel much oppress'd,
And faints for succour.
    Corin   Fair sir, I pity her,
And wish, for her sake more than for mine own,
My fortunes were more able to relieve her;
But I am shepherd to another man,
75 And do not shear the fleeces that I graze:
My master is of churlish disposition
And little recks to find the way to heaven
By doing deeds of hospitality.
Besides, his cote, his flocks, and bounds of feed
80 Are now on sale; and at our sheepcote now,
By reason of his absence, there is nothing
That you will feed on; but what is, come see,
And in my voice most welcome shall you be.
    Rosalind
What is he that shall buy his flock and pasture?
    Corin
85 That young swain that you saw here but erewhile,
That little cares for buying anything.
    Rosalind
I pray thee, if it stand with honesty,
Buy thou the cottage, pasture, and the flock,
And thou shalt have to pay for it of us.
    Celia
90 And we will mend thy wages. I like this place,
And willingly could waste my time in it.
    Corin
Assuredly the thing is to be sold:
Go with me: if you like upon report
The soil, the profit, and this kind of life,
95 I will your very faithful feeder be,
And buy it with your gold right suddenly.
                           [*Exeunt*

Act 2   Scene 5
We now meet Jaques, whom we heard
about in *Act 2* Scene 1. His satirical
wit amuses the other lords.

3 *turn :* tune.

12 *weasel :* a small, reddish-brown
animal, that steals eggs from birds'
nests, pierces them, and sucks out the
contents.
14 *ragged :* hoarse.

16 *stanzo :* the verse of a song; the
modern English is 'stanza', but the
word was new in England, and Jaques
is mocking it.

23 *that :* that which.
compliment : courtesy.
24 *dog-apes :* baboons.
26 *beggarly thanks :* thanks like a beggar.

Scene 5 *Another part of the forest*

Enter Amiens, Jaques, *and Others*

Amiens [*Sings*]
Under the greenwood tree
Who loves to lie with me,
And turn his merry note
Unto the sweet bird's throat,
5 *Come hither, come hither, come hither :*
Here shall he see
No enemy
But winter and rough weather.

Jaques
More, more, I prithee, more.
Amiens
10 It will make you melancholy, Monsieur Jaques.
Jaques
I thank it. More, I prithee, more! I can suck
melancholy out of a song as a weasel sucks eggs.
More, I prithee, more!
Amiens
My voice is ragged; I know I cannot please you.
Jaques
15 I do not desire you to please me; I do desire you
to sing. Come, more; another stanzo: call you 'em
stanzos?
Amiens
What you will, Monsieur Jaques.
Jaques
Nay, I care not for their names; they owe me
20 nothing. Will you sing?
Amiens
More at your request than to please myself.
Jaques
Well then, if ever I thank any man, I'll thank you:
but that they call compliment is like the encounter
of two dog-apes; and when a man thanks me heartily,
25 methinks I have given him a penny and he renders
me the beggarly thanks. Come, sing; and you that
will not, hold your tongues.

28   *cover* : lay the table.
     the while : meanwhile.

30   *look you* : look for you.

32   *disputable* : argumentative (see end of
     Act 2, Scene 1).

Amiens
Well, I'll end the song. Sirs, cover the while; the
duke will drink under this tree. He hath been all
30 this day to look you.

Jaques
And I have been all this day to avoid him. He is too
disputable for my company: I think of as many
matters as he, but I give heaven thanks, and make
no boast of them. Come, warble; come.

Amiens [*Sings*]
35   *Who doth ambition shun,*
     And loves to live i' the sun,
     Seeking the food he eats,
     And pleas'd with what he gets,
     Come hither, come hither, come hither :
40   *Here shall he see*
         No enemy
     But winter and rough weather.

43   *note* : tune.
44   *in . . . invention* : without using my
     imagination. Jaques implies that no
     imagination is needed for so trivial a
     song.

Jaques
I'll give you a verse to this note, that I made
yesterday in despite of my invention.

Amiens
45 And I'll sing it.

Jaques
Thus it goes:

         If it do come to pass
         That any man turn ass,
         Leaving his wealth and ease,
         A stubborn will to please,
50   *Ducdame, ducdame, ducdame :*
         Here shall he see
         Gross fools as he,
     An if he will come to me.

51   *Ducdame*. There is probably no real
     meaning for this word, which is
     certainly not Greek. Jaques uses it to
     draw the other lords round him, so
     that he can insult them in line 56.
54   *An if* : if.

Amiens
55 What's that 'ducdame'?

Jaques
'Tis a Greek invocation to call fools into a circle.

57   *rail against* : insult.
58   *the first-born of Egypt.* According to the Bible (Exodus 11), God destroyed the eldest son ('first-born') of every Egyptian family. The point of this remark is not clear.
59   *banquet* : snack, a light meal.

Act 2   Scene 6
Adam is exhausted, and Orlando comforts him.

4   *heart* : courage.
5   *comfort* : comfort yourself.
6   *uncouth* : wild.

8   *conceit* : imagination.
9   *comfortable* : comforted.
10 *presently* : immediately.

13 *said* : done.
14 *cheerly* : cheerfully.

17 *desert* : lonely place.
18 *Cheerly* : be cheerful.

Act 2   Scene 7
Duke Senior and the lords come together for a meal. Jaques tells them about Touchstone, and says that he would like to be a professional fool himself. He discusses the nature of satire with the duke. Orlando breaks in, and demands food for Adam and himself; they are entertained by the duke.
2   *like* : in the appearance of.
3   *but even now* : just this moment.

I'll go sleep if I can; if I cannot, I'll rail against all the first-born of Egypt.
      Amiens
And I'll go seek the duke: his banquet is prepared.
                          [*Exeunt in different directions*

Scene 6 *Another part of the forest*

Enter Orlando *and* Adam
      Adam
Dear master, I can go no further: O I die for food.
Here lie I down, and measure out my grave. Farewell, kind master.
      Orlando
Why, how now, Adam! no greater heart in thee?
5 Live a little; comfort a little; cheer thyself a little.
If this uncouth forest yield anything savage, I
will either be food for it, or bring it for food to thee.
Thy conceit is nearer death than thy powers. For
my sake be comfortable, hold death awhile at
10 the arm's end, I will here be with thee presently,
and if I bring thee not something to eat, I will give
thee leave to die; but if thou diest before I come,
thou art a mocker of my labour. Well said! thou
lookest cheerly, and I'll be with thee quickly. Yet
15 thou liest in the bleak air: come, I will bear thee to
some shelter, and thou shalt not die for lack of
a dinner, if there live anything in this desert.
Cheerly, good Adam.   [*Exeunt*

Scene 7 *Another part of the forest*

A table set out. Enter Duke Senior,
Amiens, Lords *dressed like Foresters*
      Duke Senior
I think he be transform'd into a beast,
For I can nowhere find him like a man.
      First Lord
My lord, he is but even now gone hence:

5   *compact of* : made up of.
      jars : discords.
6   According to medieval astronomy, the planets ('spheres') made music as they revolved. Duke Senior says that this music will become discordant before Jaques becomes musical.

11   *merrily*. Jaques does not usually look happy.

13   *A motley fool* : a fool in his professional, multicoloured costume.

16   *rail'd on* : criticized.
17   *good set terms* : elegant formal language (using the forms of classical rhetoric).

Here was he merry, hearing of a song.
   Duke Senior
5 If he, compact of jars, grow musical,
We shall have shortly discord in the spheres.
Go, seek him: tell him I would speak with him.
   First Lord
He saves my labour by his own approach.

      Enter Jaques
   Duke Senior
Why, how now, monsieur! what a life is this,
10 That your poor friends must woo your company?
What, you look merrily!
   Jaques
A fool, a fool! I met a fool i' the forest,
A motley fool; a miserable world!
As I do live by food, I met a fool;
15 Who laid him down and bask'd him in the sun,
And rail'd on Lady Fortune in good terms,
In good set terms, and yet a motley fool.

19   Fortune was said to favour fools,
but Touchstone is still waiting for his
fortune (i.e. wealth) and therefore
cannot call himself a fool.

20   *dial* : watch.
      poke : pocket.

21   *lack-lustre* : dull.

23   *wags* : goes.

29   *moral* : moralize.

30   *chanticleer* : cock.

31   *deep-contemplative* : profoundly
philosophical.

32   *sans* : without.
      Motley's the only wear : a fool's
dress is the only costume worth
wearing.

39   *remainder biscuit* : ship's biscuit,
left over at the end of the voyage.

41   *vents* : delivers.

44   *suit* : Touchstone puns on the
meanings 'plea' and 'costume'.

45-7 Provided that you clear ('weed')
your minds of all those wild ('rank')
ideas that I am wise. There is also a
pun on the other meaning of 'weed'—
a suit of clothes. No particular
meaning is intended in this word-play;
Jaques is simply having fun with
words.

48   *Withal* : as well.
      as large a charter : as free a licence.

50   *galled* : chafed.
      folly : comedy.

52   *'why'* : reason.

53-5 The man whom a fool, in his
wisdom, makes fun of, is very foolish if
he does not appear to ignore the taunt
('bob'), even though it has stung him
(made him 'smart').

'Good morrow, fool,' quoth I. 'No, sir,' quoth he,
'Call me not fool till heaven hath sent me fortune.'
20 And then he drew a dial from his poke,
And, looking on it with lack-lustre eye,
Says very wisely, 'It is ten o'clock;
Thus we may see,' quoth he, 'how the world wags:
'Tis but an hour ago since it was nine,
25 And after one hour more 'twill be eleven;
And so, from hour to hour we ripe and ripe,
And then from hour to hour we rot and rot,
And thereby hangs a tale.' When I did hear
The motley fool thus moral on the time,
30 My lungs began to crow like chanticleer,
That fools should be so deep-contemplative,
And I did laugh sans intermission
An hour by his dial. O noble fool!
A worthy fool! Motley's the only wear.
          Duke Senior
35 What fool is this?
          Jaques
O worthy fool! One that hath been a courtier,
And says, if ladies be but young and fair,
They have the gift to know it; and in his brain—
Which is as dry as the remainder biscuit
40 After a voyage—he hath strange places cramm'd
With observation, the which he vents
In mangled forms. O that I were a fool!
I am ambitious for a motley coat.
          Duke Senior
Thou shalt have one.
          Jaques   It is my only suit;
45 Provided that you weed your better judgments
Of all opinion that grows rank in them
That I am wise. I must have liberty
Withal, as large a charter as the wind,
To blow on whom I please; for so fools have:
50 And they that are most galled with my folly,
They most must laugh. And why, sir, must they so?
The 'why' is plain as way to parish church:
He that a fool doth very wisely hit
Doth very foolishly, although he smart,
55 Not to seem senseless of the bob; if not,

55-7   If he does not ignore the satire, the wise man's foolishness is exposed ('anatomiz'd'—as though it were dissected) by the random ('squandering') comments of the fool.

58   *Invest* : robe.

60-1   Jaques gives the standard defence of satire—that it acts like a medicine on a sick world. There is a pun on 'patiently' = 'like a sick person' and 'passively, without complaining'.

62   *Fie on thee* : don't be silly.

63   *for a counter* : in exchange for a worthless token.

66   *brutish sting* : animal lust.

67   *embossed* : swollen.
headed : i.e. as boils and spots come to a 'head'.

68   *licence of free foot* : free (immoral) living.

69   *disgorge* : pour out.
general world : world in general.

70   *cries out on* : attacks.

71   *tax* : accuse.
private party : individual person.

72-3   Is not pride as powerful and extensive as the sea, and grows until the basic sources ('very means') are exhausted ('weary') and run dry ('do ebb')?

75-6   The city-woman's clothes (which she carries on her 'shoulders') cost as much as those of a queen ('prince' = ruler); but she is not entitled ('unworthy') to wear such clothes.

77   *Who* : i.e. which 'city-woman'.

78   Her neighbour is just like herself.

79-81   Is there any man in humble ('basest') employment ('function') who thinks that I mean him, and who says that his fine clothes ('bravery') were not paid for by me (implying that I should mind my own business)?

81-2   In saying this, he reveals his folly to be the substance ('mettle') that I have described.

84   *do him right* : describe him correctly.

85   *free* : innocent.

86   *taxing* : criticism.

The wise man's folly is anatomiz'd
Even by the squandering glances of the fool.
Invest me in my motley; give me leave
To speak my mind, and I will through and through
60 Cleanse the foul body of th' infected world,
If they will patiently receive my medicine.

Duke Senior
Fie on thee! I can tell what thou wouldst do.

Jaques
What, for a counter, would I do, but good?

Duke Senior
Most mischievous foul sin, in chiding sin:
65 For thou thyself hast been a libertine,
As sensual as the brutish sting itself;
And all the embossed sores and headed evils,
That thou with licence of free foot hast caught,
Wouldst thou disgorge into the general world.

Jaques
70 Why, who cries out on pride,
That can therein tax any private party?
Doth it not flow as hugely as the sea,
Till that the weary very means do ebb?
What woman in the city do I name,
75 When that I say the city-woman bears
The cost of princes on unworthy shoulders?
Who can come in and say that I mean her,
When such a one as she, such is her neighbour?
Or what is he of basest function,
80 That says his bravery is not on my cost—
Thinking that I mean him—but therein suits
His folly to the mettle of my speech?
There then; how then? what then? Let me see wherein
My tongue hath wrong'd him: if it do him right,
85 Then he hath wrong'd himself; if he be free,
Why, then my taxing like a wild goose flies,
Unclaim'd of any man. But who comes here?

Enter Orlando, *with his sword drawn*

Orlando
Forbear, and eat no more.

Jaques   Why, I have eat none yet.

89 *necessity* : someone in extreme
need.

93 *civility* : good manners.

94 *touch'd my vein* : came near the
truth (as doctors have to find the vein
in order to draw blood).

96 *inland bred* : brought up in the city
(where manners should be better than
in the country).

97 *nurture* : good manners.

99 *answered* : satisfied.

100 *An* : if. Jaques probably starts
eating as he speaks this line.

102-3 Your courtesy will compel us,
more than your show of violence could
persuade us, to show courtesy.

106 *gently* : like a gentleman.

108 *countenance* : face.

109 *commandment* : authority.

110 *desert* : lonely place.
inaccessible : remote.

114 *knoll'd* : rung.

118 Let your status as gentlemen do
my pleading for me.

Orlando

Nor shalt not, till necessity be serv'd.

Jaques

90 Of what kind should this cock come of?

Duke Senior

Art thou thus bolden'd, man, by thy distress,
Or else a rude despiser of good manners,
That in civility thou seem'st so empty?

Orlando

You touch'd my vein at first: the thorny point

95 Of bare distress hath ta'en from me the show
Of smooth civility; yet am I inland bred
And know some nurture. But forbear, I say,
He dies that touches any of this fruit
Till I and my affairs are answered.

Jaques

100 An you will not be answered with reason, I must
die.

Duke Senior

What would you have? Your gentleness shall force
More than your force move us to gentleness.

Orlando

I almost die for food; and let me have it.

Duke Senior

105 Sit down and feed, and welcome to our table.

Orlando

Speak you so gently? Pardon me, I pray you:
I thought that all things had been savage here,
And therefore put I on the countenance
Of stern commandment. But whate'er you are

110 That in this desert inaccessible,
Under the shade of melancholy boughs,
Lose and neglect the creeping hours of time;
If ever you have look'd on better days,
If ever been where bells have knoll'd to church,

115 If ever sat at any good man's feast,
If ever from your eyelids wip'd a tear,
And know what 'tis to pity, and be pitied,
Let gentleness my strong enforcement be:
In the which hope I blush, and hide my sword.

Duke Senior

120 True is it that we have seen better days,
And have with holy bell been knoll'd to church,
And sat at good men's feasts, and wip'd our eyes
Of drops that sacred pity hath engender'd;
And therefore sit you down in gentleness

125 And take upon command what help we have
That to your wanting may be minister'd.

Orlando

Then but forbear your food a little while,
Whiles, like a doe, I go to find my fawn
And give it food. There is an old poor man,

130 Who after me hath many a weary step
Limp'd in pure love: till he be first suffic'd,
Oppress'd with two weak evils, age and hunger,
I will not touch a bit.

Duke Senior   Go find him out,
And we will nothing waste till you return.

Orlando

135 I thank ye; and be bless'd for your good comfort!
                                        [*Exit*

Duke Senior

Thou seest we are not all alone unhappy:
This wide and universal theatre
Presents more woeful pageants than the scene
Wherein we play in.

Jaques   All the world's a stage,

140 And all the men and women merely players:
They have their exits and their entrances;
And one man in his time plays many parts,
His acts being seven ages. At first the infant,
Mewling and puking in the nurse's arms.

145 And then the whining school-boy, with his satchel,
And shining morning face, creeping like snail
Unwillingly to school. And then the lover,
Sighing like furnace, with a woeful ballad
Made to his mistress' eyebrow. Then a soldier,

150 Full of strange oaths, and bearded like the pard,
Jealous in honour, sudden and quick in quarrel,
Seeking the bubble reputation
Even in the cannon's mouth. And then the justice,

125 *upon command* : as soon as you ask for it.
126 *wanting* : needs.
127 *forbear your food* : don't eat anything.

131 *suffic'd* : satisfied.
132 *weak evils* : evils causing weakness.

134 *waste* : consume.

135 *be bless'd* : may you be blessed.

136 *all alone* : the only people.

144 *Mewling* : crying (a cat is said to 'mew').
puking : vomiting.

149 *Made to* : on the subject of, and dedicated to.
150 *pard* : leopard.
151 *Jealous in honour* : quick to defend his honour.
sudden : impetuous.
152 *bubble reputation*. Fame is like a bubble because it is insubstantial and does not last long.
153 *justice* : magistrate.

154   *capon*: chicken (perhaps the magistrate had taken the chicken as a bribe).
156   *wise saws*: proverbs.
      modern instances: dull examples.
158   *pantaloon*: silly old man.
159   *pouch*: purse.
160-1 The breeches that he had worn when he was young, and saved carefully, are far too big now for his thin leg ('shrunk shank').
163   *his*: its (i.e. his voice's).
165   *mere oblivion*: complete forgetfulness.
166   *Sans*: without.

In fair round belly, with good capon lin'd,
155 With eyes severe, and beard of formal cut,
Full of wise saws and modern instances;
And so he plays his part. The sixth age shifts
Into the lean and slipper'd pantaloon,
With spectacles on nose and pouch on side,
160 His youthful hose, well sav'd, a world too wide
For his shrunk shank; and his big manly voice,
Turning again toward childish treble, pipes
And whistles in his sound. Last scene of all,
That ends this strange eventful history,
165 Is second childishness and mere oblivion,
Sans teeth, sans eyes, sans taste, sans everything.

Enter Orlando, *with* Adam
Duke Senior
Welcome. Set down your venerable burden,
And let him feed.
Orlando   I thank you most for him.

168   *most for*: especially for your kindness to.

Adam
So had you need:
170 I scarce can speak to thank you for myself.

170   *scarce*: hardly.

Duke Senior
Welcome; fall to: I will not trouble you
As yet, to question you about your fortunes.
Give us some music; and, good cousin, sing.

Amiens [*Sings*]
        Blow, blow, thou winter wind,
175   *Thou art not so unkind*
            As man's ingratitude;
        Thy tooth is not so keen,
        Because thou art not seen,
            Although thy breath be rude.
180 *Heigh-ho! sing, heigh-ho, unto the green holly:*
    Most friendship is feigning, most loving mere folly.
        Then heigh-ho, the holly!
        This life is most jolly.

175   *unkind*: unnatural.

179   *rude*: cruel.

Freeze, freeze, thou bitter sky,
That dost not bite so nigh
As benefits forgot :
185   *Though thou the waters warp,*
Thy sting is not so sharp
As friend remember'd not.
190   *Heigh-ho! sing, heigh-ho, unto the green holly :*
Most friendship is feigning, most loving mere
folly.
Then heigh-ho, the holly!
This life is most jolly.

Duke Senior
If that you were the good Sir Rowland's son,
195   As you have whisper'd faithfully you were,
And as mine eye doth his effigies witness
Most truly limn'd and living in your face,
Be truly welcome hither: I am the duke
That lov'd your father: the residue of your fortune,
200   Go to my cave and tell me. Good old man,
Thou art right welcome as thy master is.
Support him by the arm. Give me your hand,
And let me all your fortunes understand.   [*Exeunt*

185   *nigh :* sharply (near the bone).

187   *warp :* turn to ice.

195   *you have whisper'd.* While Amiens was singing, Orlando has told his story to Duke Senior.
196   *effigies :* likeness (the rhythm of the line demands a stress on the second syllable—'effìgies').
197   *limn'd :* painted.
199   *residue of your fortune :* rest of your history.
201   *right :* very.

Act 3

Duke Frederick orders Oliver to find
Orlando, and takes his possessions
from him.

2   If I were not for the most part made
of mercy.
3   *absent argument :* subject (for revenge)
who is not here—i.e. Orlando.
4   *thou present :* when you are here.
6   *with candle :* i.e. by night as well as by
day; the expression comes from
St. Luke's Gospel 15:8.
7   *turn :* return.

10   *Worth seizure ·* worth taking.
11   *quit :* acquit.
mouth : evidence.

13   *my heart :* my real feelings.

16   *of such a nature :* experienced in these
things.
17   *extent upon :* valuation of.
18   *expediently :* quickly.
turn him going : send him on his way.

Act 3   Scene 2
Orlando hangs his poem on a tree.
Corin and Touchstone debate the
merits of the country life and court
life. Rosalind reads Orlando's verses,
then she and Celia talk about Orlando.
Orlando comes on to the scene, and
Rosalind (who of course is dressed as
a man) teases him about his love, and
offers to cure him of it.

Scene 1 *A room in the palace*

Enter Duke Frederick, Oliver, Lords, *and*
Attendants
Duke Frederick
Not see him since! Sir, sir, that cannot be:
But were I not the better part made mercy,
I should not seek an absent argument
Of my revenge, thou present. But look to it:
5 Find out thy brother, wheresoe'er he is;
Seek him with candle; bring him, dead or living,
Within this twelvemonth, or turn thou no more
To seek a living in our territory.
Thy lands and all things that thou dost call thine
10 Worth seizure, do we seize into our hands,
Till thou canst quit thee by thy brother's mouth
Of what we think against thee.
Oliver
O that your highness knew my heart in this!
I never lov'd my brother in my life.
Duke Frederick
15 More villain thou. Well, push him out of doors;
And let my officers of such a nature
Make an extent upon his house and lands.
Do this expediently, and turn him going.   [*Exeunt*

Scene 2 *The Forest of Arden*

Enter Orlando, *with a paper, which he
fixes on a tree*
Orlando
Hang there, my verse, in witness of my love; A
And thou, thrice-crowned queen of night, survey B
With thy chaste eye, from thy pale sphere above, A
Thy huntress' name, that my full life doth sway. B

2   *thrice-crowned queen of night :*
Luna, the moon-goddess in Greek and
Roman mythology. She was also
Diana, goddess of chastity and
hunting; and Proserpina, goddess of
the underworld.

4   *Thy huntress' name :* i.e. the name of
Rosalind, whom Orlando imagines to
be one of the virgins who
accompanied Diana in her hunting.
   full : whole.
   sway : rule.

6   *character :* inscribe.

8   *witness'd :* spoken of.

10   *unexpressive she :* woman that no
words can describe.

13-21 Touchstone intends to bewilder
Corin by listing qualities which are
really identical but which are made to
sound as though they were opposites.

14   *naught :* worthless.

16   *private :* cut off from the world.

19   *spare :* frugal.
   humour : appetite.

22-9 Corin is playing Touchstone's
own game, and offering as his
'philosophy' various truisms (ideas
whose truth is very obvious).

23   *wants :* lacks.

28-9 *complain of :* complain that he
lacks.

30   *natural :* by nature; Touchstone
puns on the meaning 'fool'.

---

5 O Rosalind! these trees shall be my books,
And in their barks my thoughts I'll character,
That every eye, which in this forest looks,
Shall see thy virtue witness'd everywhere.
10 Run, run, Orlando: carve on every tree
The fair, the chaste, and unexpressive she.   [*Exit*

Enter Corin *and* Touchstone

Corin
And how like you this shepherd's life, Master
Touchstone?

Touchstone
Truly, shepherd, in respect of itself, it is a good life;
but in respect that it is a shepherd's life, it is naught.
15 In respect that it is solitary, I like it very well; but
in respect that it is private, it is a very vile life. Now,
in respect it is in the fields, it pleaseth me well; but
in respect it is not in the court, it is tedious. As it is
a spare life, look you, it fits my humour well; but as
20 there is no more plenty in it, it goes much against my
stomach. Hast any philosophy in thee, shepherd?

Corin
No more but that I know the more one sickens, the
worse at ease he is; and that he that wants money,
means, and content, is without three good friends;
25 that the property of rain is to wet, and fire to burn;
that good pasture makes fat sheep; and that a great
cause of the night is lack of the sun; that he that
hath learned no wit by nature nor art may complain
of good breeding, or comes of a very dull kindred.

Touchstone
30 Such a one is a natural philosopher. Wast ever in
court, shepherd?

Corin
No, truly.

Touchstone
Then thou art damned.

Corin
Nay, I hope.

Touchstone
35 Truly, thou art damned, like an ill-roasted egg, all
on one side.

Corin

For not being at court? Your reason.

Touchstone

Why, if thou never wast at court, thou never sawest
good manners; if thou never sawest good manners,
40 then thy manners must be wicked; and wickedness
is sin, and sin is damnation. Thou art in a parlous
state, shepherd.

Corin

Not a whit, Touchstone: those that are good
manners at the court, are as ridiculous in the country
45 as the behaviour of the country is most mockable at
the court. You told me you salute not at the court,
but you kiss your hands: that courtesy would be
uncleanly if courtiers were shepherds.

Touchstone

Instance, briefly; come, instance.

Corin

50 Why, we are still handling our ewes, and their fells,
you know, are greasy.

Touchstone

Why, do not your courtier's hands sweat? and is not
the grease of a mutton as wholesome as the sweat of
a man? Shallow, shallow. A better instance, I say;
55 come.

39   *good manners.* Touchstone first uses
this phrase in the sense 'politeness',
and then twists his sentence so that
the second meaning is 'good conduct'.

41   *parlous :* perilous.

43   *Not a whit :* not at all.

46-7   *you salute . . . hands :* you do not
greet anyone at court without kissing
hands.

49   *Instance :* give me proof of that.

50   *still :* constantly.
        fells : fleeces.

52   *your :* any.

Corin
Besides, our hands are hard.

Touchstone
Your lips will feel them the sooner: shallow again.
A more sounder instance; come.

Corin
And they are often tarred over with the surgery of
60 our sheep; and would you have us kiss tar? The
courtier's hands are perfumed with civet.

Touchstone
Most shallow man! Thou worms-meat, in respect
of a good piece of flesh, indeed! Learn of the wise,
and perpend: civet is of a baser birth than tar, the
65 very uncleanly flux of a cat. Mend the instance,
shepherd.

Corin
You have too courtly a wit for me: I'll rest.

Touchstone
Wilt thou rest damned? God help thee, shallow
man! God make incision in thee! thou art raw.

Corin
70 Sir, I am a true labourer: I earn that I eat, get that
I wear, owe no man hate, envy no man's happiness,
glad of other men's good, content with my harm;
and the greatest of my pride is to see my ewes graze
and my lambs suck.

Touchstone
75 That is another simple sin in you, to bring the ewes
and the rams together, and to offer to get your living
by the copulation of cattle; to be bawd to a bell-
wether, and to betray a she-lamb of a twelvemonth
to a crooked-pated, old, cuckoldy ram, out of all
80 reasonable match. If thou be'st not damned for this,
the devil himself will have no shepherds: I cannot
see else how thou shouldst 'scape.

Corin
Here comes young Master Ganymede, my new
mistress's brother.

Enter Rosalind, *reading a paper*

Rosalind
85 From the east to western Ind,
No jewel is like Rosalind.

---

59   *surgery.* Tar was used to cover wounds on sheep.

61   *civet :* a secretion ('flux') from the glands of the civet cat, used in making perfume.

62-3   *Thou . . . flesh :* you are only fit to be eaten by worms, compared with a proper man.

64   *perpend :* consider (Touchstone's word is very pompous)

65   *Mend :* improve.

67   *rest :* give up.

69   May God cut you in slices (so that you can be cooked better).
raw. Touchstone puns on the meanings 'uneducated' and 'uncooked'.

70   *that :* that which.
get : earn.

72   *content with my harm :* patient with my own sufferings.

75   *simple.* Touchstone puns on the meanings 'foolish' and 'unashamed'.

76   *offer :* dare.

77   *bawd :* pander.
bell-wether : the leader of a flock of sheep, which carried a bell round its neck so that the other sheep would hear and follow.

78   *of a twelvemonth :* yearling.

79   *crooked-pated :* with crooked horns. Horns were a symbol of the husband whose wife was unfaithful to him— i.e. a 'cuckold'. See illustration, p. 75.

79-80   *out . . . match :* in a most unsuitable marriage.

80-1   *If . . . shepherds :* if you are not damned for this, it is because the devil refuses to accept shepherds in hell.

82   *'scape :* escape damnation.

85   *Ind :* Indies.

87-8   The report of her merits is blown through the world by the wind.

89   *lin'd* : drawn.

90   *to* : compared with.

91   *kept in mind* : remembered.

94-5   *it is . . . market* : it is just the jogging rhythm of women on their way to market to sell butter.

96   *Out* : be quiet.

97   *For a taste* : as a sample.

98-109   Touchstone makes a bawdy parody of Orlando's rhymes.

100-1   Just as the cat goes after its mate, so does Rosalind.

102   *lin'd* : given a warm lining; the word also meant 'mated'.

104-5   People must carry every act to its logical conclusion. When they have reaped the corn, they must gather it into sheaves, bind the sheaves, and load them on to the cart. Rosalind must also be 'carted'—tied to a cart and whipped; this was the punishment for prostitutes.

106   *rind* : shell.

110   *This . . . verses* : exactly the uncomfortable pace (neither trot nor gallop) of his verses.

114   *graff* : engraft.

115   *medlar* : a kind of apple which is not fit for eating until it is over-ripe. Rosalind puns on 'meddler' = 'an interfering person', and says that Touchstone will be dead ('rotten') before his mind is mature ('ripe').

117   *right virtue* : true quality.

Her worth, being mounted on the wind,
Through all the world bears Rosalind.
90   All the pictures fairest lin'd
Are but black to Rosalind.
Let no face be kept in mind,
But the fair of Rosalind.

Touchstone
I'll rhyme you so, eight years together, dinners and suppers and sleeping hours excepted; it is the right
95   butter-women's rank to market.

Rosalind
Out, fool!

Touchstone
For a taste:

If a hart do lack a hind,
Let him seek out Rosalind.
100   If the cat will after kind,
So be sure will Rosalind.
Winter-garments must be lin'd,
So must slender Rosalind.
They that reap must sheaf and bind,
105   Then to cart with Rosalind.
Sweetest nut hath sourest rind,
Such a nut is Rosalind.
He that sweetest rose will find
Must find love's prick and Rosalind.

110   This is the very false gallop of verses: why do you infect yourself with them?

Rosalind
Peace, you dull fool: I found them on a tree.

Touchstone
Truly, the tree yields bad fruit.

Rosalind
I'll graff it with you, and then I shall graff it with
115   a medlar: then it will be the earliest fruit i' the country; for you'll be rotten ere you be half ripe, and that's the right virtue of the medlar.

Touchstone
You have said; but whether wisely or no, let the forest judge.

Enter Celia, *reading a paper*

Rosalind

120 Peace!
Here comes my sister, reading: stand aside.

Celia

Why should this a desert be?
    For it is unpeopled? No;
Tongues I'll hang on every tree,
125   That shall civil sayings show.
Some, how brief the life of man
    Runs his erring pilgrimage,
That the stretching of a span
    Buckles in his sum of age;
130 Some, of violated vows
    'Twixt the souls of friend and friend:
But upon the fairest boughs,
    Or at every sentence end,
Will I 'Rosalinda' write;
135   Teaching all that read to know
The quintessence of every sprite
    Heaven would in little show.
Therefore Heaven Nature charg'd
    That one body should be fill'd
140 With all graces wide enlarg'd:
    Nature presently distill'd
Helen's cheek, but not her heart,
    Cleopatra's majesty,
Atalanta's better part,
145   Sad Lucretia's modesty.
Thus Rosalind of many parts
    By heavenly synod was devis'd,
Of many faces, eyes, and hearts,
    To have the touches dearest priz'd.
150 Heaven would that she these gifts should have,
And I to live and die her slave.

Rosalind

O most gentle Jupiter! what tedious homily of love
have you wearied your parishioners withal, and
never cried, 'Have patience, good people!'

Celia

155 How now? back, friends! Shepherd, go off a little.
Go with him, sirrah.

122   *desert :* lonely place.
123   *For :* because.

127   *erring :* wandering.
128   *span :* width of stretched hand
measured between the tips of the
thumb and the little finger.
129   *Buckles in :* encloses.
        sum of age : length of life.

136   *quintessence :* the purest form.
        sprite : spirit.
137   *in little :* contracted into a small
space—i.e. into Rosalind.
138-40   Heaven ordered Nature to fill a
single body (Rosalind's) with all the
graces that were scattered ('enlarg'd')
among the whole world ('wide').
141   *presently :* at once.
142   The beauty of Helen of Troy,
but not her heart (Helen was
faithless).
144   Atalanta was a princess in Greek
mythology who compelled her suitors
to run a race with her; she always won,
and the defeated suitors were
condemned to death. Her 'better part'
was her speed in running.
145   Lucrece killed herself after she
had been raped by Tarquin;
Shakespeare's poem *The Rape of
Lucrece* tells the story.
146   *of :* from.
147   *synod :* council.
149   *touches :* details.
150   *would :* wished.
152   *Jupiter :* king of the gods in
classical mythology.

158   *bag and baggage* : a colloquial
       phrase, still used, meaning 'with all our
       belongings'—i.e. the bag and all it
       contains; Touchstone puns on
       'baggage' meaning 'a cheeky young
       woman'.
158-9 *scrip and scrippage* : wallet and all
       it contains; Touchstone invents
       'scrippage' to match 'baggage'.
161-7 Celia and Rosalind play with the
       meanings of 'feet' (feet in a line of
       verse, *and* the body's feet) and 'bear'
       (carry, *and* endure).

166   *without* : outside.

169   *should be* : came to be.

171   Rosalind refers to the phrase
       'a nine days' wonder' (meaning
       'a short-lived surprise'), and says that
       she has almost recovered from her
       amazement.
173   *palm-tree.* The Forest of Arden is
       an imaginary place, so there is no need
       to wonder whether palm-trees ever
       grew in England.
174-5 Rosalind claims to have been a rat
       at the time of Pythagoras, the Greek
       philosopher who believed that souls
       were transmitted from one form of
       animal life to another. As an 'Irish
       rat', she had been killed by ritual
       incantation; it was a common joke in
       England at the time of Shakespeare
       that the Irish claimed to rid themselves
       of rats (and other enemies) in this way.
176   *Trow you* : do you know.
181   *friends* : lovers.
183   *encounter* : i.e. the lovers may
       encounter each other.

Touchstone

Come, shepherd, let us make an honourable retreat;
though not with bag and baggage, yet with scrip
and scrippage.   [*Exeunt* Corin *and* Touchstone

Celia

160 Didst thou hear these verses?

Rosalind

O, yes, I heard them all, and more too; for some of
them had in them more feet than the verses would
bear.

Celia

That's no matter: the feet might bear the verses.

Rosalind

165 Ay, but the feet were lame, and could not bear
themselves without the verse, and therefore stood
lamely in the verse.

Celia

But didst thou hear without wondering, how thy
name should be hanged and carved upon these
170 trees?

Rosalind

I was seven of the nine days out of the wonder
before you came; for look here what I found on
a palm-tree. I was never so be-rhymed since
Pythagoras' time, that I was an Irish rat, which
175 I can hardly remember.

Celia

Trow you who hath done this?

Rosalind

Is it a man?

Celia

And a chain, that you once wore, about his neck.
Change you colour?

Rosalind

180 I prithee, who?

Celia

O Lord, Lord! it is a hard matter for friends to
meet; but mountains may be removed with earth-
quakes, and so encounter.

Rosalind

Nay, but who is it?

186   *petitionary vehemence* : passionate begging.

190   *out of all whooping* : beyond all expression of surprise.

191   *Good my complexion* : spare my blushes.

192   *caparisoned* : dressed.

192-3   *I have . . . disposition* : I have a masculine nature.

194   *a South Sea of discovery* : as long and frustrating as a voyage of exploration in the South Seas.
       prithee : pray you.

195   *apace* : fast.
       would : wish.

200   *tidings* : news.

201   If you will swallow my news, then you will have a man in your stomach.

206   *stay* : wait for.

210-11   *sad . . . maid* : with a serious face, and as an honest girl.

Celia
185 Is it possible?

Rosalind
Nay, I prithee now, with most petitionary vehemence, tell me who it is.

Celia
O wonderful, wonderful, and most wonderful wonderful! and yet again wonderful! and after that,
190 out of all whooping!

Rosalind
Good my complexion! dost thou think though I am caparisoned like a man, I have a doublet and hose in my disposition? One inch of delay more is a South Sea of discovery; I prithee, tell me who is
195 it quickly, and speak apace. I would thou couldst stammer, that thou mightst pour this concealed man out of thy mouth, as wine comes out of a narrow-mouthed bottle; either too much at once, or none at all. I prithee, take the cork out of thy
200 mouth, that I may drink thy tidings.

Celia
So you may put a man in your belly.

Rosalind
Is he of God's making? What manner of man? Is his head worth a hat, or his chin worth a beard?

Celia
Nay, he hath but a little beard.

Rosalind
205 Why, God will send more, if the man will be thankful. Let me stay the growth of his beard, if thou delay me not the knowledge of his chin.

Celia
It is young Orlando, that tripped up the wrestler's heels and your heart, both in an instant.

Rosalind
210 Nay, but the devil take mocking! speak, sad brow and true maid.

Celia
I' faith, coz, 'tis he.

Rosalind
Orlando?

Celia
Orlando.

217 *Wherein went he :* what was he wearing?

217-18 *What makes he :* what is he doing?

218 *Where remains he :* where is he now?

221 *Gargantua :* a giant, who once swallowed five pilgrims in a single mouthful; the creation of the 16th century French writer, Rabelais.

223 *particulars :* questions.
is more than : would take more time than it takes.

226 *freshly :* attractive.

228 *atomies :* specks of dust.
resolve : answer.
propositions : problems.

229 *take a taste :* enjoy (as though it were a meal).

230 *relish . . . observance :* add sauce to it by listening carefully.

231 *acorn :* the nut of the oak tree, which was sacred to Jupiter ('Jove').

234 *audience :* hearing.

237-8 *it well . . . ground :* it is a most fitting decoration for the earth.

239 *holla :* stop.
curvets : leaps around.

240 *unseasonably :* at the wrong time.
furnish'd : dressed.

241 *heart.* Rosalind puns on 'heart' and 'hart'.

242 *would :* wish I could.
burden : accompaniment.

Rosalind

215 Alas the day! what shall I do with my doublet and hose? What did he when thou sawest him? What said he? How looked he? Wherein went he? What makes he here? Did he ask for me? Where remains he? How parted he with thee, and when shalt thou
220 see him again? Answer me in one word.

Celia

You must borrow me Gargantua's mouth first: 'tis a word too great for any mouth of this age's size. To say 'ay' and 'no' to these particulars is more than to answer in a catechism.

Rosalind

225 But doth he know that I am in this forest and in man's apparel? Looks he as freshly as he did the day he wrestled?

Celia

It is as easy to count atomies as to resolve the propositions of a lover; but take a taste of my finding
230 him, and relish it with good observance. I found him under a tree, like a dropped acorn.

Rosalind

It may well be called Jove's tree, when it drops forth such fruit.

Celia

Give me audience, good madam.

Rosalind

235 Proceed.

Celia

There lay he, stretched along like a wounded knight.

Rosalind

Though it be pity to see such a sight, it well becomes the ground.

Celia

Cry 'holla' to thy tongue, I prithee; it curvets
240 unseasonably. He was furnish'd like a hunter.

Rosalind

O, ominous! he comes to kill my heart.

Celia

I would sing my song without a burden: thou bringest me out of tune.

Rosalind

Do you not know I am a woman? when I think,
245 I must speak. Sweet, say on.

Celia

246 *bring me out* : put me off.

You bring me out. Soft! comes he not here?

Rosalind

'Tis he: slink by, and note him.

Enter Orlando *and* Jaques

Jaques

I thank you for your company; but, good faith,
I had as lief have been myself alone.

249 *as lief* : rather.

Orlando

250 And so had I; but yet, for fashion' sake, I thank
you too for your society.

Jaqucs

252 *God buy you* : God be with you.

God buy you: let's meet as little as we can.

Orlando

253 *better strangers* : i.e. not, as usual,
'better friends'.

I do desire we may be better strangers.

Jaques

I pray you, mar no more trees with writing love-
255 songs in their barks.

Orlando

I pray you, mar no more of my verses with reading
them ill-favouredly.

257 *ill-favouredly* : badly.

Jaques

Rosalind is your love's name?

Orlando

Yes, just.

259 *just* : indeed.

Jaques

260 I do not like her name.

Orlando

There was no thought of pleasing you when she
was christened.

Jaques

What stature is she of?

Orlando

Just as high as my heart.

Jaques

265-7 The 'goldsmiths' wives' could
have shown Orlando the rings that
their husbands made, which would
have verses engraved inside them;
Orlando could have learned ('conn'd')
these by heart.

265 You are full of pretty answers. Have you not been
acquainted with goldsmiths' wives, and conn'd
them out of rings?

268-9 I learned my answers from the
       same place that you learned your
       questions—painted wall-hangings.
       (Such imitation tapestry was used in
       inns; the painted figures had balloons,
       with words in them, coming from their
       mouths.)
271   *Atalanta's heels.* See note on
       3, 1, 144.
272   *rail against :* swear at.
274   *breather :* man who breathes.

277   *change :* exchange.

279   *troth :* faith.

284   *cipher :* the figure 'o', i.e. nothing.

290   *lackey :* servant.
       under that habit : in that
       appearance.
       play the knave : trick.
292   *what would you :* what do you
       want?

Orlando
Not so; but I answer you right painted cloth, from
whence you have studied your questions.

Jaques
270 You have a nimble wit: I think 'twas made of
Atalanta's heels. Will you sit down with me? and
we two will rail against our mistress the world, and
all our misery.

Orlando
I will chide no breather in the world but myself,
275 against whom I know most faults.

Jaques
The worst fault you have is to be in love.

Orlando
'Tis a fault I will not change for your best virtue.
I am weary of you.

Jaques
By my troth, I was seeking for a fool when I found
280 you.

Orlando
He is drowned in the brook: look but in, and you
shall see him.

Jaques
There I shall see mine own figure.

Orlando
Which I take to be either a fool or a cipher.

Jaques
285 I'll tarry no longer with you. Farewell, good Signior
Love.

Orlando
I am glad of your departure. Adieu, good Monsieur
Melancholy.   [*Exit* Jaques

Rosalind
[*Aside to Celia*] I will speak to him like a saucy
290 lackey, and under that habit play the knave with
him. Do you hear, forester?

Orlando
Very well: what would you?

Rosalind
I pray you, what is't o'clock?

Orlando
You should ask me, what time o' day; there's no
295 clock in the forest.

Rosalind

Then there is no true lover in the forest; else sighing every minute and groaning every hour would detect the lazy foot of Time as well as a clock.

Orlando

300 And why not the swift foot of Time? had not that been as proper?

Rosalind

By no means, sir. Time travels in divers paces with divers persons. I'll tell you who Time ambles withal, who Time trots withal, who Time gallops withal, and who he stands still withal.

Orlando

305 I prithee, who doth he trot withal?

Rosalind

Marry, he trots hard with a young maid between the contract of her marriage and the day it is solemnized; if the interim be but a sev'nnight, Time's pace is so hard that it seems the length of 310 seven year.

Orlando

Who ambles Time withal?

Rosalind

With a priest that lacks Latin, and a rich man that hath not the gout; for the one sleeps easily because he cannot study, and the other lives merrily because 315 he feels no pain; the one lacking the burden of lean and wasteful learning, the other knowing no burden of heavy tedious penury. These Time ambles withal.

Orlando

Who doth he gallop withal?

Rosalind

320 With a thief to the gallows; for though he go as softly as foot can fall, he thinks himself too soon there.

Orlando

Who stays it still withal?

Rosalind

With lawyers in the vacation; for they sleep between 325 term and term, and then they perceive not how Time moves.

300 *proper*: appropriate.

301 *divers*: different.

303 *withal*: with.

306 *trots hard*. Hard trotting is an uncomfortable pace.
307-8 The marriage 'contract' was an exchange of promises to marry; it was more formal and binding than a modern 'engagement', but it did not allow the couple to consummate their union until this had been 'solemnized' by the church ceremony.
308 *interim*: interval.
      sev'nnight: week.

315-16 *lean . . . learning*: study that makes a man go thin and waste away.

320-1 *go as softly*: walk as slowly.

324 *vacation*. The law-courts in England keep the same terms and vacations as the universities.

328   *skirts :* outskirts.

331   *cony :* rabbit.
       kindled : born.

333   *purchase :* acquire.
       removed : remote.

334   *of :* by.
335   *religious :* i.e. member of some
       religious order.
336   *inland :* cultured, educated in
       civilized places.
337   *courtship :* life at court *and*
       wooing.
338   *read :* deliver.
339   *touched with :* guilty of.
340   *generally :* the female sex in
       general.
       taxed : accused.
343   *laid . . . women :* accused
       women of.

346   *his :* its.

348–9 I will only give advice to those
       who need it (Rosalind's metaphor
       comes from St. Matthew's Gospel
       9:12).
349   *haunts :* frequents.
352   *forsooth :* indeed.
       deifying : making a god out of.
353   *fancy-monger :* dealer in love
       (Rosalind invents the word, on the
       pattern of 'fishmonger').
355   *quotidian :* malarial fever, one of
       whose symptoms was a continuous
       shivering.
356   *love-shaked :* shaken by the fever
       of love.

Orlando
Where dwell you, pretty youth?
Rosalind
With this shepherdess, my sister; here in the skirts
of the forest, like fringe upon a petticoat.
Orlando
330 Are you native of this place?
Rosalind
As the cony, that you see dwell where she is kindled.
Orlando
Your accent is something finer than you could
purchase in so removed a dwelling.
Rosalind
I have been told so of many: but indeed an old
335 religious uncle of mine taught me to speak, who
was in his youth an inland man; one that knew
courtship too well, for there he fell in love. I have
heard him read many lectures against it; and I
thank God I am not a woman, to be touched with
340 so many giddy offences as he hath generally taxed
their whole sex withal.
Orlando
Can you remember any of the principal evils that
he laid to the charge of women?
Rosalind
There were none principal; they were all like one
345 another as halfpence are; every one fault seeming
monstrous till his fellow fault came to match it.
Orlando
I prithee, recount some of them.
Rosalind
No, I will not cast away my physic but on those
that are sick. There is a man haunts the forest, that
350 abuses our young plants with carving 'Rosalind'
on their barks; hangs odes upon hawthorns, and
elegies on brambles; all, forsooth, deifying the
name of Rosalind: if I could meet that fancy-
monger, I would give him some good counsel, for
355 he seems to have the quotidian of love upon him.
Orlando
I am he that is so love-shaked. I pray you, tell me
your remedy.

358   *my uncle's marks :* the symptoms which my uncle described.

359–60   *cage of rushes :* i.e. a prison from which it is easy to escape.

362   *a blue eye :* dark rings round the eyes.

363   *unquestionable :* apathetic.

366   *your having :* what you possess.

367   *revenue :* income.

368   *unbanded :* without a ribbon.

370   *a careless desolation :* a despair that makes you careless of your appearance.

371   *point-device :* to the point of perfection.

372   *accoutrements :* attire.

372–3   *as . . . other :* you look more like a man who loves himself than the lover of another person.

374   *would :* wish.

Rosalind

There is none of my uncle's marks upon you: he taught me how to know a man in love; in which cage
360 of rushes I am sure you are not prisoner.

Orlando

What were his marks?

Rosalind

A lean cheek, which you have not; a blue eye and sunken, which you have not; an unquestionable spirit, which you have not; a beard neglected,
365 which you have not—but I pardon you for that, for, simply, your having in beard is a younger brother's revenue. Then, your hose should be ungartered, your bonnet unbanded, your sleeve unbuttoned, your shoe untied, and everything about you
370 demonstrating a careless desolation. But you are no such man: you are rather point-device in your accoutrements; as loving yourself than seeming the lover of any other.

Orlando

Fair youth, I would I could make thee believe I
375 love.

377   *apter :* more likely.

379   *still :* always.
         give . . . consciences : lie about
their real feelings.
380   *sooth :* truth.

388   *a dark . . . whip.* This was the
usual treatment, in Elizabethan times,
for madmen, who were thought to be
possessed of the devil. If the devil
could be whipped out, then the
madmen would be cured.
391   *profess curing :* claim to cure.
         counsel : advice.

396   *moonish :* changeable (influenced
by the moon).
397   *fantastical :* fanciful.
         apish : affected.
398-400 *for every . . . anything :* showing
signs of every emotion, but feeling no
emotion sincerely.
401   *cattle of this colour :* creatures of
this kind.
402   *entertain him :* receive him
kindly.
         forswear : refuse.
403   *that :* with the result that.
         drave : drove.
404   *humour :* mood.
405   *forswear :* renounce.
406-7   *a nook merely monastic :* a place
remote from the world and completely
without women.
408   *liver :* the seat of all passions (as
the Elizabethans thought).

Rosalind

Me believe it! you may as soon make her that you
love believe it; which, I warrant, she is apter to do
than to confess she does; that is one of the points in
the which women still give the lie to their con-
380 sciences. But, in good sooth, are you he that hangs
the verses on the trees, wherein Rosalind is so
admired?

Orlando

I swear to thee, youth, by the white hand of
Rosalind, I am that he, that unfortunate he.

Rosalind

385 But are you so much in love as your rhymes speak?

Orlando

Neither rhyme nor reason can express how much.

Rosalind

Love is merely a madness, and, I tell you, deserves
as well a dark house and a whip as madmen do; and
the reason why they are not so punished and cured
390 is, that the lunacy is so ordinary that the whippers
are in love too. Yet I profess curing it by counsel.

Orlando

Did you ever cure any so?

Rosalind

Yes, one; and in this manner. He was to imagine
me his love, his mistress; and I set him every day
395 to woo me: at which time would I, being but a
moonish youth, grieve, be effeminate, changeable,
longing and liking; proud, fantastical, apish,
shallow, inconstant, full of tears, full of smiles, for
every passion something, and for no passion truly
400 anything, as boys and women are, for the most part,
cattle of this colour; would now like him, now
loathe him; then entertain him, then forswear him;
now weep for him, then spit at him; that I drave
my suitor from his mad humour of love to a living
405 humour of madness, which was, to forswear the
full stream of the world, and to live in a nook merely
monastic. And thus I cured him; and this way will
I take upon me to wash your liver as clean as a sound
sheep's heart, that there shall not be one spot of
410 love in 't.

411 *would not :* do not want to be.

413 *cote :* cottage.

416-17 *by the way :* on the way.

Orlando
I would not be cured, youth.
Rosalind
I would cure you, if you would but call me Rosalind, and come every day to my cote and woo me.
Orlando
Now, by the faith of my love, I will: tell me where
415 it is.
Rosalind
Go with me to it and I'll show it you; and by the way you shall tell me where in the forest you live. Will you go?
Orlando
With all my heart, good youth.
Rosalind
420 Nay, you must call me Rosalind. Come, sister, will you go?   *[Exeunt*

Act 3 Scene 3
Touchstone is about to marry Audrey, a simple country girl whom he has met in the Forest. Jaques, however, thinks that the marriage is not being properly performed, so he persuades them to give more thought to the subject.

1 *apace :* quickly.
2 *the man :* i.e. that you have chosen to marry.
3 *yet :* still.
   feature : person.
4 *warrant :* defend.
5-6 Touchstone is enjoying sophisticated word-play here, but the joke is quite lost on Audrey. There is a pun on 'goats' and 'Goths'; Ovid, a Roman poet, was in exile among the Goths (barbarians), just as Touchstone is among the goats. The original meaning of 'capricious' is 'goat-like', and 'goat-like' means 'lustful'—a better description of Ovid, who wrote very erotic verse, than 'honest'.
7 *ill-inhabited :* poorly housed.
7-8 *Jove . . . house.* The king of the classical gods lived for a time in a poor cottage when he was entertained by two peasants, Baucis and Philemon.

Scene 3 *Another part of the forest*

Enter Touchstone *and* Audrey; Jaques *behind them*
Touchstone
Come apace, good Audrey: I will fetch up your goats, Audrey. And now, Audrey? am I the man yet? doth my simple feature content you?
Audrey
Your features! Lord warrant us, what features?
Touchstone
5 I am here with thee and thy goats, as the most capricious poet, honest Ovid, was among the Goths.
Jaques
[*Aside*] O knowledge ill-inhabited, worse than Jove in a thatched house!
Touchstone
When a man's verse cannot be understood, nor a
10 man's good wit seconded with the forward child, understanding, it strikes a man more dead than a great reckoning in a little room. Truly, I would the gods had made thee poetical.

10   *seconded with* : supported by.
      forward : intelligent.
11   *understanding* : i.e. the listener's
      understanding.
12   *a great . . . room.* This line does not
      make much sense *unless* it is read as
      Shakespeare's allusion to the death of
      Christopher Marlowe, his only rival as
      a poet and dramatist, who was killed in
      1593 during a fight in a lodging-house;
      the fight was said to be caused by an
      argument over who should pay the bill
      —the 'reckoning'.
16   *the . . . feigning* : the truest poetry
      is the most false—i.e. the best poetry
      is the most imaginative.
17   *given to* : in the habit of writing.
18   *feign* : pretend.

25   *hard-favoured* : ugly.
26-7 *honey . . . sugar* : i.e. too much of a
      good thing.

28   *A material fool* : a fool with a lot of
      ideas.

33   *foul* : plain; Audrey is glad to be
      plain because she hopes this will keep
      her virtuous.

39   *couple* : join.

40   *fain* : would like to.

Audrey
I do not know what 'poetical' is. Is it honest in
15 deed and word? Is it a true thing?
Touchstone
No, truly, for the truest poetry is the most feigning;
and lovers are given to poetry, and what they swear
in poetry may be said as lovers they do feign.
Audrey
Do you wish then that the gods had made me
20 poetical?
Touchstone
I do, truly; for thou swearest to me thou art
honest: now, if thou wert a poet, I might have some
hope thou didst feign.
Audrey
Would you not have me honest?
Touchstone
25 No, truly, unless thou wert hard-favoured; for
honesty coupled to beauty is to have honey a sauce
to sugar.
Jaques
[*Aside*] A material fool.
Audrey
Well, I am not fair, and therefore I pray the gods
30 make me honest.
Touchstone
Truly, and to cast away honesty upon a foul slut
were to put good meat into an unclean dish.
Audrey
I am not a slut, though I thank the gods I am foul.
Touchstone
Well, praised be the gods for thy foulness! sluttish-
35 ness may come hereafter. But be it as it may be,
I will marry thee; and to that end I have been with
Sir Oliver Martext, the vicar of the next village,
who hath promised to meet me in this place of the
forest, and to couple us.
Jaques
40 [*Aside*] I would fain see this meeting.
Audrey
Well, the gods give us joy!

43   *stagger* : stumble.

44   *horn-beasts* : animals (such as deer) with horns; this leads Touchstone to meditate on horns as the symbol for cuckolds (men whose wives have been unfaithful to them).

45   *what though* : what does it matter?

46-7 *no end . . . goods* : the full amount of his possessions.

47   *good horns* : good cause to wear horns (be a cuckold).

48   *knows . . . them* : does not know how faithless his wife is.

49   *dowry* : the money (or goods) a wife brings to her husband when she marries.

50   *Poor men alone* : is it only poor men who are made cuckolds?

51   *rascal* : inferior animal in a herd.

52   *walled* : surrounded by a city wall.

55-7 It is better to be able to defend oneself than to have no skill with a sword, and in the same way it is better to have a faithless wife than no wife at all.

58   *Sir Oliver Martext*. 'Sir' was the usual title given to clergymen. The name 'Martext' suggests that there is something wrong with this parson; he will 'mar' (spoil) a text.

59   *dispatch* : deal with.

61   *to give the woman*. The question asked in the marriage ceremony is 'Who giveth this woman to be married to this man', and it is usual for the bride's father to reply 'I do'.

66   *What-ye-call't*. Touchstone pretends to have forgotten the name—or else pretends that he is reluctant to say the word 'Jaques'; this is pronounced 'jakes', which is a word for the lavatory—the English are still shy about asking for this.

67   *God 'ild you* : God reward you.

68   *last company* : latest act of companionship (i.e. coming forward at this time).

   even : just.

69   *toy* : trifle.

   pray be covered : put your hat on (Jaques has taken off his hat out of respect for the parson and the

Touchstone
Amen. A man may, if he were of a fearful heart, stagger in this attempt; for here we have no temple but the wood, no assembly but horn-beasts. But
45 what though? Courage! As horns are odious, they are necessary. It is said, 'many a man knows no end of his goods.' Right! Many a man has good horns, and knows no end of them. Well, that is the dowry of his wife; 'tis none of his own getting. Horns?
50 Even so. Poor men alone? No, no; the noblest deer hath them as huge as the rascal. Is the single man therefore blessed? No: as a walled town is more worthier than a village, so is the forehead of a married man more honourable than the bare brow of a
55 bachelor; and by how much defence is better than no skill, by so much is a horn more precious than to want. Here comes Sir Oliver.

   Enter Sir Oliver Martext
Sir Oliver Martext, you are well met: will you dispatch us here under this tree, or shall we go
60 with you to your chapel?

Sir Oliver Martext
Is there none here to give the woman?

Touchstone
I will not take her on gift of any man.

Sir Oliver Martext
Truly, she must be given, or the marriage is not lawful.

Jaques
65 [*Coming forward*] Proceed, proceed: I'll give her.

Touchstone
Good even, good Master What-ye-call't: how do you, sir? You are very well met: God 'ild you for your last company: I am very glad to see you: even a toy in hand here, sir: nay, pray be covered.

Jaques
70 Will you be married, motley?

Touchstone
As the ox hath his bow, sir, the horse his curb, and the falcon her bells, so man hath his desires; and as pigeons bill, so wedlock would be nibbling.

occasion, but Touchstone assumes that the respect is for himself).

70   *motley :* fool.
71   *bow :* yoke.
      curb : bit.
72   *bells :* they were tied to the falcon's legs to help the owner to catch his bird.
      man . . . desires : just as various animals have restrictions put upon them, so man is restricted by his desires.
73   *bill :* caress each other with their beaks (bills).
78   *wainscot :* wood panelling on walls.
79   *green :* unseasoned.
      warp : lose shape.
81   *not in the mind but :* inclined to think that.
82   *of :* by.
      like : likely.
87   *in bawdry :* in sin.

89   *O sweet Oliver.* Touchstone sings three lines from a popular song, and then parodies them.

92   *Wind away :* go on your way.

96   *fantastical :* clever.
97   *flout :* mock.
      calling : vocation.

Act 3   Scene 4
Rosalind talks about Orlando, the man she loves, and Celia teases her. Corin comes to tell them that they may overhear Phebe's cruelty to Silvius.

1   *Never :* don't.

2   *I prithee :* I pray you.

3   *become :* suit.

Jaques
And will you, being a man of your breeding, be
75 married under a bush, like a beggar? Get you to
church, and have a good priest that can tell you
what marriage is: this fellow will but join you
together as they join wainscot; then one of you will
prove a shrunk panel, and like green timber, warp,
80 warp.
        Touchstone
[*Aside*] I am not in the mind but I were better to be
married of him than of another: for he is not like to
marry me well, and not being well married, it will
be a good excuse for me hereafter to leave my wife.
        Jaques
85 Go thou with me, and let me counsel thee.
        Touchstone
Come, sweet Audrey:
We must be married, or we must live in bawdry.
Farewell, good Master Oliver: not

            O sweet Oliver!
90   O brave Oliver!
        Leave me not behind thee:
but
            Wind away,
            Begone, I say,
95   I will not to wedding with thee.

            [*Exeunt* Jaques, Touchstone, *and* Audrey
        Sir Oliver Martext
'Tis no matter: ne'er a fantastical knave of them all
shall flout me out of my calling.   [*Exit*

Scene 4 *Another part of the forest*

        Enter Rosalind *and* Celia
        Rosalind
Never talk to me: I will weep.
        Celia
Do, I prithee; but yet have the grace to consider
that tears do not become a man.

6 *dissembling colour :* deceitful colour, i.e. red, which was (by tradition) the colour of Judas's hair.
7 *Something :* a little.
7–8 *his kisses . . . children :* his kisses are like those of Judas (who betrayed Christ with a kiss).

10 *your :* the.

13 *holy bread :* bread used in the Communion Service.

14 *cast :* discarded.
Diana : goddess of virginity.
15 *winter's sisterhood :* complete chastity.

21 *pick-purse :* thief who steals purses.
22 *verity :* truth.
23 *concave :* hollow.
covered goblet : drinking vessel covered with a hollow lid to show that it was empty.

26 *in :* i.e. in love.

27 *downright :* plainly.

29 *tapster :* waiter at an inn.

Rosalind
But have I not cause to weep?
Celia
5 As good cause as one would desire; therefore weep.
Rosalind
His very hair is of the dissembling colour.
Celia
Something browner than Judas's; marry, his kisses are Judas's own children.
Rosalind
I' faith, his hair is of a good colour.
Celia
10 An excellent colour: your chestnut was ever the only colour.
Rosalind
And his kissing is as full of sanctity as the touch of holy bread.
Celia
He hath bought a pair of cast lips of Diana: a nun
15 of winter's sisterhood kisses not more religiously; the very ice of chastity is in them.
Rosalind
But why did he swear he would come this morning, and comes not?
Celia
Nay, certainly, there is no truth in him.
Rosalind
20 Do you think so?
Celia
Yes: I think he is not a pick-purse nor a horse-stealer; but for his verity in love, I do think him as concave as a covered goblet or a worm-eaten nut.
Rosalind
25 Not true in love?
Celia
Yes, when he is in; but I think he is not in.
Rosalind
You have heard him swear downright he was.
Celia
'Was' is not 'is': besides, the oath of a lover is no stronger than the word of a tapster; they are both

30   *confirmer . . . reckonings :* witnesses to false statements.

32   *question :* conversation.

37-41   All Orlando's fine ('brave') protestations of love go across his lover's heart, just as an inexperienced ('puisny') competitor in a tilting match, by spurring his horse on one side only, breaks his lance ('staff'), and makes a fool ('goose') of himself.

42   *all's brave . . . guides :* all love, that is ruled by youth and guided by folly, is fine.

30   the confirmer of false reckonings. He attends here in the forest on the duke your father.

Rosalind

I met the duke yesterday and had much question with him. He asked me of what parentage I was; I told him, of as good as he; so he laughed, and let

35 me go. But what talk we of fathers, when there is such a man as Orlando?

Celia

O, that's a brave man! he writes brave verses, speaks brave words, swears brave oaths, and breaks them bravely, quite traverse, athwart the heart of

40 his lover; as a puisny tilter, that spurs his horse but on one side, breaks his staff like a noble goose. But all's brave that youth mounts and folly guides. Who comes here?

Enter Corin

Corin

Mistress and master, you have oft inquir'd

45 After the shepherd that complain'd of love,
Who you saw sitting by me on the turf,
Praising the proud disdainful shepherdess
That was his mistress.

Celia   Well, and what of him?

49 *pageant* : spectacle.

53 *mark* : watch.
     remove : move on.

Corin
If you will see a pageant truly play'd,
50 Between the pale complexion of true love
And the red glow of scorn and proud disdain,
Go hence a little, and I shall conduct you,
If you will mark it.
        Rosalind   O come, let us remove:
The sight of lovers feedeth those in love.
55 Bring us to this sight, and you shall say
I'll prove a busy actor in their play.   [*Exeunt*

Act 3   Scene 5
Silvius pleads with Phebe, but she
refuses to believe in his romantic love,
and mocks him. Rosalind, dressed as
Ganymede, speaks sharply to Phebe,
and tells her that she does not deserve
to be loved. But Phebe suddenly falls
in love with 'Ganymede'.

4   Whose heart is made hard because he
is accustomed to seeing death.

5   *Falls* : lets fall

6   In Elizabethan England the executioner used to ask the prisoner's
forgiveness before he executed him.

Scene 5 *Another part of the forest*

Enter Silvius *and* Phebe
        Silvius
Sweet Phebe, do not scorn me; do not, Phebe:
Say that you love me not, but say not so
In bitterness. The common executioner,
Whose heart the accustom'd sight of death makes
        hard,
5 Falls not the axe upon the humbled neck
But first begs pardon: will you sterner be
Than he that dies and lives by bloody drops?

Enter Rosalind, Celia, *and* Corin, *behind*
        Phebe
I would not be thy executioner:
I fly thee, for I would not injure thee.

10 *murder in mine eye*. It was a cliché of
romantic love that the loved one's eyes
could kill with a glance.

11 This is a pretty idea, to be sure; and
it is very likely (Phebe is being
sarcastic here).

13 *atomies* : specks of dust.

19 *Lie not* : do not tell lies.

10 Thou tell'st me there is murder in mine eye:
'Tis pretty, sure, and very probable,
That eyes, that are the frail'st and softest things,
Who shut their coward gates on atomies,
Should be call'd tyrants, butchers, murderers!
15 Now I do frown on thee with all my heart;
And, if mine eyes can wound, now let them kill
        thee;
Now counterfeit to swoon; why, now fall down;
Or, if thou canst not, O for shame, for shame,
Lie not, to say mine eyes are murderers.
20 Now show the wound mine eye hath made in thee;
Scratch thee but with a pin, and there remains
Some scar of it; lean but upon a rush,

23   *cicatrice :* scar.
      capable impressure : impression that
      it bears.
25   *darted :* thrown like darts.

29   *power of fancy :* power to draw your
      love.

31   *love's keen arrows.* Cupid, the classical
      god of love, was traditionally pictured
      with bow and arrows.

38-9 *I see . . . bed :* I cannot see any
      beauty in you that would light up a
      dark bedroom without a candle
      (another commonplace of romantic
      love).
42-3 *than . . . sale-work :* than in the
      ordinary goods that nature makes for
      a quick sale.
43   *'Od's :* may God save.
44   *tangle :* entangle.

47   *bugle :* bead (made of black glass).
48   *entame :* enslave.
      to your worship : to worship you.
50   *foggy south :* south-west wind.
51   *properer :* more handsome.
52   *such fools as you :* i.e. who love plain
      women.
53   *ill-favour'd :* plain.
54   *glass :* looking-glass.
55   *out of you :* looking out of you (as
      out of a mirror).
      proper : attractive.

The cicatrice and capable impressure
Thy palm some moment keeps; but now mine eyes,
25 Which I have darted at thee, hurt thee not,
Nor, I am sure, there is no force in eyes
That can do hurt.
          Silvius   O dear Phebe,
If ever, as that ever may be near,
You meet in some fresh cheek the power of fancy,
30 Then shall you know the wounds invisible
That love's keen arrows make.
          Phebe   But, till that time
Come not thou near me; and, when that time
   comes,
Afflict me with thy mocks, pity me not;
As, till that time, I shall not pity thee.
          Rosalind
35 [*Advancing*] And why, I pray you? Who might be
      your mother,
That you insult, exult, and all at once,
Over the wretched? What though you have no
      beauty—
As by my faith, I see no more in you
Than without candle may go dark to bed—
40 Must you be therefore proud and pitiless?
Why, what means this? Why do you look on me?
I see no more in you than in the ordinary
Of nature's sale-work. 'Od's my little life!
I think she means to tangle my eyes too.
45 No, faith, proud mistress, hope not after it:
'Tis not your inky brows, your black silk hair,
Your bugle eyeballs, nor your cheek of cream,
That can entame my spirits to your worship.
You foolish shepherd, wherefore do you follow her,
50 Like foggy south, puffing with wind and rain?
You are a thousand times a properer man
Than she a woman: 'tis such fools as you
That make the world full of ill-favour'd children:
'Tis not her glass, but you, that flatters her;
55 And out of you she sees herself more proper
Than any of her lineaments can show her.
But, mistress, know yourself: down on your knees,
And thank heaven, fasting, for a good man's love:

For I must tell you friendly in your ear,

60 Sell when you can; you are not for all markets.
Cry the man mercy; love him; take his offer:
Foul is most foul, being foul to be a scoffer.
So take her to thee, shepherd. Fare you well.

Phebe
Sweet youth, I pray you, chide a year together:

65 I had rather hear you chide than this man woo.

Rosalind
He's fallen in love with your foulness, and she'll
fall in love with my anger. If it be so, as fast as she
answers thee with frowning looks, I'll sauce her
with bitter words. Why look you so upon me?

Phebe
70 For no ill will I bear you.

Rosalind
I pray you, do not fall in love with me,
For I am falser than vows made in wine.
Besides, I like you not. If you will know my house,
'Tis at the tuft of olives, here hard by.

75 Will you go, sister? Shepherd, ply her hard.
Come, sister. Shepherdess, look on him better,
And be not proud: though all the world could see,
None could be so abus'd in sight as he.
Come, to our flock.

[*Exeunt* Rosalind, Celia, *and* Corin

Phebe
80 Dead shepherd, now I find thy saw of might:
'Who ever lov'd that lov'd not at first sight?'

Silvius
Sweet Phebe—

Phebe   Ha! what say'st thou, Silvius?

Silvius
Sweet Phebe, pity me.

Phebe
Why, I am sorry for thee, gentle Silvius.

Silvius
85 Wherever sorrow is, relief would be:
If you do sorrow at my grief in love,
By giving love, your sorrow and my grief
Were both extermin'd.

---

60   Accept Silvius's offer of marriage; you won't always find someone who wants you.

61   *Cry ... mercy* : beg for his forgiveness.

62   Ugliness is most ugly when the ugly person ('being foul') is also disdainful ('a scoffer').

64   *a year together* : a year without stopping.

68   *sauce* : make her smart.

70   *ill will* : dislike.

72   *in wine* : when one is drunk.

74   *here hard by* : very near here.

75   *ply her hard* : persuade her forcefully.

77–8   *though ... he* : if all the world could see her, no-one would be so mistaken by the sight as he is.

80   *Dead shepherd*. Another reference to Christopher Marlowe (see *3, 3, 12*); it is conventional that in a pastoral setting he should be called a 'shepherd'. The line that follows this one comes from Marlowe's poem *Hero and Leander*.
    saw : saying.
    of might : is very true.

85   When you feel sorry for someone, you want to help that person.

88   *extermin'd* : destroyed.

89   *neighbourly*. Phebe refers to the
second commandment of Jesus, 'Thou
shalt love thy neighbour as thyself'
(St. Matthew's Gospel 22:39).

90   *that were :* that would be.
covetousness. The tenth commandment of Moses is 'Thou shalt not
covet' (Exodus 20:17).

91   *the time was :* once upon a time.

92   *yet it is not :* even now it is not
true.

94   *erst :* formerly.
irksome : a nuisance.

96   *recompense :* reward.

99   *poverty of grace :* in such a need of
your favour.

100-3   Silvius has cast himself in the role
of Ruth, who asked her mother 'Let
me now go to the field, and glean ears
of corn after him in whose sight I shall
find grace' (The Book of Ruth 2:2).

104   *erewhile :* just now.

106   *bounds :* land.

107   *carlot :* farmer (Shakespeare seems
to have invented this word).

113   *becomes :* suits.

114   *proper :* handsome.

118   *so-so :* passable.

120   *lusty :* vivid.

Phebe
Thou hast my love: is not that neighbourly?
Silvius
90 I would have you.
Phebe   Why, that were covetousness.
Silvius, the time was that I hated thee;
And yet it is not that I bear thee love:
But since that thou canst talk of love so well,
Thy company, which erst was irksome to me,
95 I will endure, and I'll employ thee too;
But do not look for further recompense
Than thine own gladness that thou art employ'd.
Silvius
So holy and so perfect is my love,
And I in such a poverty of grace,
100 That I shall think it a most plenteous crop
To glean the broken ears after the man
That the main harvest reaps: loose now and then
A scatter'd smile, and that I'll live upon.
Phebe
Know'st thou the youth that spoke to me erewhile?
Silvius
105 Not very well, but I have met him oft;
And he hath bought the cottage and the bounds
That the old carlot once was master of.
Phebe
Think not I love him, though I ask for him.
'Tis but a peevish boy; yet he talks well;
110 But what care I for words? yet words do well,
When he that speaks them pleases those that hear.
It is a pretty youth: not very pretty.
But, sure, he's proud; and yet his pride becomes
    him.
He'll make a proper man. The best thing in him
115 Is his complexion; and faster than his tongue
Did make offence, his eye did heal it up.
He is not very tall; yet for his years he's tall.
His leg is but so-so; and yet 'tis well.
There was a pretty redness in his lip,
120 A little riper and more lusty red
    Than that mix'd in his cheek; 'twas just the
    difference

122   *mingled damask :* mixed red and
      white; we still speak of 'damask roses'.
123   *mark'd :* observed.

124   *In parcels :* bit by bit.

128   *what . . . to do :* what right had he?

130   *I am remember'd :* I remember.

132   *that's all one :* that doesn't matter.
      omittance is no quittance : because I
      failed to rebuke him, it does not mean
      that I have pardoned him.

135   *straight :* at once.

137   *passing short :* very brief.

Betwixt the constant red and mingled damask.
There be some women, Silvius, had they mark'd
    him
In parcels as I did, would have gone near
125 To fall in love with him; but, for my part,
I love him not, nor hate him not; and yet
I have more cause to hate him than to love him:
For what had he to do to chide at me?
He said mine eyes were black and my hair black;
130 And, now I am remember'd, scorn'd at me.
I marvel why I answer'd not again:
But that's all one; omittance is no quittance.
I'll write to him a very taunting letter,
And thou shalt bear it: wilt thou, Silvius?
          Silvius
135 Phebe, with all my heart.
          Phebe   I'll write it straight;
The matter's in my head and in my heart:
I will be bitter with him and passing short.
Go with me, Silvius.   [*Exeunt*

Act 4

Act 4　Scene 1
Rosalind, dressed as Ganymede, holds
a witty conversation with Jaques.
Orlando arrives. He pretends that
Ganymede is his Rosalind, and swears
that he loves her and wants to marry
her. When he has gone, Celia
reproaches Rosalind (in fun) for being
shameless.

6　　*modern :* commonplace; they make
themselves an obvious target for
reproach.

8　　*sad :* serious.

11　　*emulation :* (professional) jealousy.
fantastical : fanciful, tempera-
mental.
14　　*politic :* crafty.
nice : fastidious.
15-16　*melancholy . . . simples :* my
melancholy is like a medicine, made up
('compounded') from many herbs
('simples').
16-18　*extracted . . . travels :* taken from
many things that I have seen and the
different ('sundry') things that I have
thought about (contemplated) on my
travels.
18-19　*in which . . . sadness :* musing
('rumination') about them frequently
wraps me in a very moody
('humorous') sadness.

Scene 1 *The Forest of Arden*

Enter Rosalind, Celia, *and* Jaques

Jaques
I prithee, pretty youth, let me be better acquainted
with thee.
Rosalind
They say you are a melancholy fellow.
Jaques
I am so; I do love it better than laughing.
Rosalind
5　Those that are in extremity of either are abominable
fellows, and betray themselves to every modern
censure worse than drunkards.
Jaques
Why, 'tis good to be sad and say nothing.
Rosalind
Why then, 'tis good to be a post.
Jaques
10　I have neither the scholar's melancholy, which is
emulation; nor the musician's, which is fantastical;
nor the courtier's, which is proud; nor the soldier's,
which is ambitious; nor the lawyer's, which is
politic; nor the lady's, which is nice; nor the lover's,
15　which is all these: but it is a melancholy of mine
own, compounded of many simples, extracted from
many objects, and indeed the sundry contemplation
of my travels, in which my often rumination wraps
me in a most humorous sadness.
Rosalind
20　A traveller! By my faith, you have great reason to
be sad. I fear you have sold your own lands to see
other men's; then, to have seen much and to have
nothing, is to have rich eyes and poor hands.

Jaques

Yes, I have gained my experience.

Rosalind

25 And your experience makes you sad: I had rather
have a fool to make me merry than experience to
make me sad: and to travel for it too!

Enter Orlando

Orlando

Good day, and happiness, dear Rosalind!

Jaques

Nay then, God buy you, an you talk in blank verse.

[*Exit*

Rosalind

30 Farewell, Monsieur Traveller: look you lisp, and
wear strange suits, disable all the benefits of your
own country, be out of love with your nativity, and
almost chide God for making you that countenance
you are; or I will scarce think you have swam in a
35 gondola. Why, how now, Orlando! where have you
been all this while? You a lover! An you serve me
such another trick, never come in my sight more.

Orlando

My fair Rosalind, I come within an hour of my
promise.

Rosalind

40 Break an hour's promise in love! He that will
divide a minute into a thousand parts, and break
but a part of the thousandth part of a minute in the
affairs of love, it may be said of him that Cupid hath
clapped him o' the shoulder, but I'll warrant him
45 heart-whole.

Orlando

Pardon me, dear Rosalind.

Rosalind

Nay, an you be so tardy, come no more in my sight:
I had as lief be wooed of a snail.

Orlando

Of a snail!

Rosalind

50 Ay, of a snail; for though he comes slowly, he
carries his house on his head; a better jointure,
I think, than you make a woman: besides, he brings
his destiny with him.

24   *gained*: paid for.

29   *God buy you*: God be with you.
     an: if.
     talk in blank verse. Touchstone
     recognizes that the change from prose
     to blank verse (the medium of most
     poetic drama) indicates the arrival of
     one of the romantic lovers and the
     renewal of the romantic love theme.
30   *lisp*. speak with a foreign accent.
31   *strange suits*: costumes of other
     countries.
     disable: belittle.
32   *nativity*: nationality.
34–5 *swam in a gondola*: i.e. been
     abroad; gondolas are the means of
     transport through the canals of Venice.
36   *An*: if.

43–4 *Cupid . . . shoulder*: Cupid has
     arrested him (like a policeman).
44   *warrant*: guarantee.
45   *heart-whole*: innocent.

47   *tardy*: late.
48   *as lief*: rather.

51   *jointure*: marriage-settlement (in
     this case, a house).

Orlando

What's that?

Rosalind

55 Why, horns; which such as you are fain to be beholding to your wives for: but he comes armed in his fortune and prevents the slander of his wife.

Orlando

Virtue is no horn-maker; and my Rosalind is virtuous.

Rosalind

60 And I am your Rosalind?

Celia

It pleases him to call you so; but he hath a Rosalind of a better leer than you.

Rosalind

Come, woo me, woo me; for now I am in a holiday humour, and like enough to consent. What would

65 you say to me now, an I were your very very Rosalind?

Orlando

I would kiss before I spoke.

Rosalind

Nay, you were better speak first, and when you were gravelled for lack of matter, you might take

70 occasion to kiss. Very good orators, when they are out, they will spit; and for lovers lacking—God warn us!—matter, the cleanliest shift is to kiss.

Orlando

How if the kiss be denied?

Rosalind

Then she puts you to entreaty, and there begins

75 new matter.

Orlando

Who could be out, being before his beloved mistress?

Rosalind

Marry, that should you, if I were your mistress; or I should think my honesty ranker than my wit.

Orlando

80 What, of my suit?

Rosalind

Not out of your apparel, and yet out of your suit. Am not I your Rosalind?

---

55   *horns.* See illustration, p. 75.
     are fain to be: must be.
56-7 *he comes . . . wife:* he is already equipped with what he must inevitably acquire later, and so anticipates ('prevents') the disgrace which his wife will bring to him.
58   *horn-maker:* maker of cuckolds.

62   *leer:* complexion.

64   *humour:* mood.
     like enough: very likely.
65   *an:* if.

69   *gravelled:* stuck (like a boat that has run on to sand).
70   *occasion:* opportunity.
71   *out:* at a loss for words.
71-2 *God warn us:* God protect us (i.e. it is not very likely that this could happen).
72   *cleanliest shift:* quickest way out.
74   *to entreaty:* to plead with her.

76   *out:* at a loss for words.

79   *ranker:* stronger; if Rosalind's wit is stronger than her modesty, she will be clever enough to keep a young man in his place (out of his suit).
81   Not out of your clothes, yet out of your courtship. There is a pun on two meanings of 'suit'—'clothes' and 'courtship'.

Orlando

I take some joy to say you are, because I would be talking of her.

Rosalind

85 Well, in her person I say I will not have you.

Orlando

Then in mine own person I die.

Rosalind

No, faith, die by attorney. The poor world is almost six thousand years old, and in all this time there was not any man died in his own person, 90 *videlicet*, in a love-cause. Troilus had his brains dashed out with a Grecian club; yet he did what he could to die before, and he is one of the patterns of love. Leander, he would have lived many a fair year, though Hero had turned nun, if it had not been for 95 a hot midsummer night; for, good youth, he went but forth to wash him in the Hellespont, and being taken with the cramp was drowned; and the foolish chroniclers of that age found it was 'Hero of Sestos'. But these are all lies: men have died from time to 100 time, and worms have eaten them, but not for love.

Orlando

I would not have my right Rosalind of this mind; for, I protest, her frown might kill me.

Rosalind

By this hand, it will not kill a fly. But come, now I will be your Rosalind in a more coming-on disposi-105 tion; and ask me what you will, I will grant it.

Orlando

Then love me, Rosalind.

Rosalind

Yes, faith will I, Fridays and Saturdays and all.

Orlando

And wilt thou have me?

Rosalind

Ay, and twenty such.

Orlando

110 What sayest thou?

Rosalind

Are you not good?

---

85   *in her person* : on her behalf.

87   *by attorney* : by having someone else, usually a lawyer ('attorney') act on one's behalf.

90   *videlicet* : namely (a legal term).
   Troilus : a Trojan prince in love with Cressida, a Greek, at the time of the Trojan War. Cressida was unfaithful, but Troilus did not die of love; instead he was killed in battle. Shakespeare tells the story in his play *Troilus and Cressida.*

93   *Leander* : he fell in love with Hero, a priestess ('nun') of the temple of Venus in Sestos. Leander lived at Abydos, on the other side of the Hellespont, and swam over to meet Hero. One night there was a storm, and Leander was drowned. The story is told in Marlowe's poem *Hero and Leander.*

98   *it* : the cause of death.

101 *right* : true.
   of this mind : of the same opinion.

104 *coming-on* : approachable.

Orlando

I hope so.

Rosalind

Why then, can one desire too much of a good thing?
—Come, sister, you shall be the priest and marry
115 us.—Give me your hand, Orlando. What do you
say, sister?

Orlando

Pray thee, marry us.

Celia

I cannot say the words.

Rosalind

You must begin—'Will you, Orlando'—

Celia

120 Go to. Will you, Orlando, have to wife this
Rosalind?

Orlando

I will.

Rosalind

Ay, but when?

Orlando

Why now; as fast as she can marry us.

Rosalind

125 Then you must say, 'I take thee, Rosalind, for wife.'

Orlando

I take thee, Rosalind, for wife.

Rosalind

I might ask you for your commission; but, I do take
thee, Orlando, for my husband: there's a girl goes
before the priest; and, certainly, a woman's thought
130 runs before her actions.

Orlando

So do all thoughts; they are winged.

Rosalind

Now tell me how long you would have her after you
have possessed her?

Orlando

For ever and a day.

Rosalind

135 Say 'a day', without the 'ever'. No, no, Orlando;
men are April when they woo, December when
they wed: maids are May when they are maids,

120   *Go to :* Stop it!

127   *commission :* authority. See
Introduction, p. xx.
128-9   *goes before :* anticipates.

139   *Barbary* : North African.
140–1 *against rain* : before it rains.
141   *new-fangled* : always wanting some-
       thing new.
       giddy : changeable.
143   *Diana* : the goddess of chastity;
       her statue was placed in fountains as an
       allusion to the story that Actaeon spied
       on her while she was bathing, and was
       changed into a stag for his
       impertinence.
145   *hyen* : hyena.

150   *the waywarder* : the more wilful.
       Make : close
151   *casement* : window.

155   *Wit, whither wilt* : wit, where are
       you going. This was a catchword of the
       time, often used to check a talkative
       person; see *1*, *2*, *34*.

159   *Marry* : by the Virgin Mary.

162   *her husband's occasion* : a chance to
       find fault with her husband.
163   *breed* : rear.

but the sky changes when they are wives. I will be
more jealous of thee than a Barbary cock-pigeon
140 over his hen; more clamorous than a parrot against
rain; more new-fangled than an ape; more giddy in
my desires than a monkey: I will weep for nothing,
like Diana in the fountain, and I will do that when
you are disposed to be merry; I will laugh like a
145 hyen, and that when thou art inclined to sleep.

Orlando
But will my Rosalind do so?

Rosalind
By my life, she will do as I do.

Orlando
O but she is wise.

Rosalind
Or else she could not have the wit to do this: the
150 wiser, the waywarder. Make the doors upon a
woman's wit, and it will out at the casement; shut
that, and 'twill out at the key-hole; stop that, 'twill
fly with the smoke out at the chimney.

Orlando
A man that had a wife with such a wit, he might
155 say, 'Wit, whither wilt?'

Rosalind
Nay, you might keep that check for it till you met
your wife's wit going to your neighbour's bed.

Orlando
And what wit could wit have to excuse that?

Rosalind
Marry, to say she came to seek you there. You shall
160 never take her without her answer, unless you take
her without her tongue. O that woman that cannot
make her fault her husband's occasion, let her never
nurse her child herself, for she will breed it like a
fool.

Orlando
165 For these two hours, Rosalind, I will leave thee.

Rosalind
Alas, dear love, I cannot lack thee two hours.

Orlando
I must attend the duke at dinner: by two o'clock
I will be with thee again.

Rosalind

Ay, go your ways, go your ways; I knew what
170 you would prove, my friends told me as much, and
I thought no less: that flattering tongue of yours
won me: 'tis but one cast away, and so, come,
death! Two o'clock is your hour?

Orlando

Ay, sweet Rosalind.

Rosalind

175 By my troth, and in good earnest, and so God mend
me, and by all pretty oaths that are not dangerous,
if you break one jot of your promise or come one
minute behind your hour, I will think you the most
pathetical break-promise, and the most hollow
180 lover, and the most unworthy of her you call
Rosalind, that may be chosen out of the gross band
of the unfaithful. Therefore, beware my censure,
and keep your promise.

Orlando

With no less religion than if thou wert indeed my
185 Rosalind: so, adieu.

Rosalind

Well, Time is the old justice that examines all
such offenders, and let Time try. Adieu.

[*Exit* Orlando

Celia

You have simply misused our sex in your love-
prate: we must have your doublet and hose plucked
190 over your head, and show the world what the bird
hath done to her own nest.

Rosalind

O coz, coz, coz, my pretty little coz, that thou didst
know how many fathom deep I am in love! But it
cannot be sounded: my affection hath an unknown
195 bottom, like the Bay of Portugal.

Celia

Or rather, bottomless; that as fast as you pour
affection in, it runs out.

Rosalind

No; that same wicked bastard of Venus, that was
begot of thought, conceived of spleen, and born of
200 madness, that blind rascally boy that abuses every-

172   *one cast away :* one woman disposed of.

175   *troth :* faith.
        in good earnest : in all seriousness.

179   *pathetical :* miserable.

181   *gross :* total.

187   *try :* be the judge.

188   *simply :* utterly.
        misused : disgraced.
        love-prate : lovers' chatter.
189-90 *plucked over your head :* stripped off you. This phrase was used when servants lost their jobs and were stripped of their uniforms.
190-1   *bird . . . nest.* There is a common saying—'it is a foul bird that defiles its own nest'.
194   *sounded :* measured.

198   *bastard of Venus :* Cupid; he was the son of Venus and her lover, Mercury (and not her husband, Vulcan).
199   *thought :* fancy.
        spleen : impulse.

201   *his own.* Cupid is represented without eyes, to signify that love is blind.

204   *a shadow :* some shade.

one's eyes because his own are out, let him be judge how deep I am in love. I'll tell thee, Aliena, I cannot be out of the sight of Orlando : I'll go find a shadow, and sigh till he come.

Celia

205 And I'll sleep.   [*Exeunt*

Act 4   Scene 2

The lords have been hunting and killed a deer. This scene accounts for the two hours which must pass before Orlando can come to Rosalind again.

Scene 2 *Another part of the forest*

Enter Jaques, *and* Lords *dressed as Foresters*

Jaques

Which is he that killed the deer?

First Lord

Sir, it was I.

Jaques

3-4   *like a Roman conqueror :* i.e. with a wreath on his head.

5   *branch of victory :* the deer's horns, which are said to 'branch', will serve for the conqueror's wreath.

Let's present him to the duke, like a Roman conqueror; and it would do well to set the deer's horns upon his head for a branch of victory. Have you no song, forester, for this purpose?

Second Lord

Yes, sir.

Jaques

Sing it: 'tis no matter how it be in tune so it make
noise enough.

Song

10   *What shall he have that kill'd the deer?*
        His leather skin and horns to wear.
            Then sing him home.
        Take thou no scorn to wear the horn;
        It was a crest ere thou wast born:
15   *Thy father's father wore it,*
            And thy father bore it:
        The horn, the horn, the lusty horn
        Is not a thing to laugh to scorn.   [*Exeunt*

13   Don't be ashamed to wear horns
        (i.e. be a cuckold with an unfaithful
        wife).

Scene 3 *Another part of the forest*

Enter Rosalind *and* Celia

Rosalind

How say you now? Is it not past two o'clock?
And here much Orlando!

Celia

I warrant you, with pure love and troubled brain,
he hath ta'en his bow and arrows, and is gone forth
5 to sleep. Look, who comes here.

Enter Silvius

Silvius

My errand is to you, fair youth.
My gentle Phebe did bid me give you this:
                              [*Giving a letter*
I know not the contents; but, as I guess
By the stern brow and waspish action
10 Which she did use as she was writing of it,
It bears an angry tenor: pardon me;
I am but as a guiltless messenger.

Rosalind

[*Reading the letter*] Patience herself would startle
    at this letter,

Act 4   Scene 3
Orlando is late. Silvius comes to Celia
and Rosalind (who is still dressed as
Ganymede), bringing a letter from
Phebe. Rosalind is scornful, and reads
the letter, in which Phebe declares
her love. As soon as Silvius has gone,
Oliver, whom we have not seen for a
long time, comes in search of
Ganymede. He recounts an adventure
where Orlando has been brave and
generous. When she hears that he has
been wounded, Rosalind faints.

2   *much Orlando:* a lot we see of
        Orlando (Rosalind is ironic).

4-5   *he hath . . . sleep:* he went out
        hunting and fell asleep.

11   *tenor:* message.

12   *but as:* only.

13-14   *startle at:* be startled by.

14 *play the swaggerer*: be ready to fight.
bear this, bear all: if I can endure
this, I can endure anything.
16 *and that*: and says that.
17 *phoenix*: a legendary Arabian bird;
only one existed at any time, and when
the old phoenix died on a funeral pyre,
its successor rose from the ashes.
'Od's my will: as God's will is my
will.
20 *device*: invention.

23 *turn'd into*: brought into.

25 *freestone*: greyish yellow sandstone.
verily: in truth.

29 *hand*: handwriting.

34 *giant-rude*: extremely impertinent.
35 *Ethiop*: Ethiopian.

39 *She Phebes me*: she writes to me in
her own style.

42 *rail*: scold.

44 *laid apart*: set aside for a time.

And play the swaggerer: bear this, bear all:
15 She says I am not fair; that I lack manners;
She calls me proud, and that she could not love me
Were man as rare as phoenix. 'Od's my will!
Her love is not the hare that I do hunt:
Why writes she so to me? Well, shepherd, well,
20 This is a letter of your own device.
     Silvius
No, I protest, I know not the contents:
Phebe did write it.
     Rosalind   Come, come, you are a fool,
And turn'd into the extremity of love.
I saw her hand: she has a leathern hand,
25 A freestone-colour'd hand; I verily did think
That her old gloves were on, but 'twas her hands:
She has a housewife's hand; but that's no matter:
I say she never did invent this letter;
This is a man's invention, and his hand.
     Silvius
30 Sure, it is hers.
     Rosalind
Why, 'tis a boisterous and a cruel style,
A style for challengers; why, she defies me,
Like Turk to Christian: women's gentle brain
Could not drop forth such giant-rude invention,
35 Such Ethiop words, blacker in their effect
Than in their countenance. Will you hear the letter?
     Silvius
So please you, for I never heard it yet;
Yet heard too much of Phebe's cruelty.
     Rosalind
She Phebes me. Mark how the tyrant writes.
[*Reads*]
40   Art thou god to shepherd turn'd,
       That a maiden's heart hath burn'd?

Can a woman rail thus?
     Silvius
Call you this railing?
     Rosalind
[*Reads*]
       Why, thy godhead laid apart,
45   Warr'st thou with a woman's heart?

Did you ever hear such railing?
> Whiles the eye of man did woo me,
> That could do no vengeance to me,
Meaning me a beast.

47-8 So long as it was a human eye that courted me, it could do me no harm.

50   *eyne* : eyes.

50 If the scorn of your bright eyne
Have power to raise such love in mine,
Alack! in me what strange effect
Would they work in mild aspect.
Whiles you chid me, I did love;

53   *mild aspect* : favourably (the phrase is taken from astrology).
54   *Whiles* : when.

55 How then might your prayers move!
He that brings this love to thee
Little knows this love in me;
And by him seal up thy mind;
Whether that thy youth and kind

58   Send a sealed letter by him, telling me what you think.
59   *kind* : nature.
61   *make* : bring (i.e. bring a dowry).

60 Will the faithful offer take
Of me and all that I can make;
Or else by him my love deny,
And then I'll study how to die.

Silvius
Call you this chiding?

Celia
65 Alas, poor shepherd!

Rosalind
Do you pity him? no, he deserves no pity. Wilt thou love such a woman? What, to make thee an instrument and play false strains upon thee! not to be endured! Well, go your way to her, for I see love
70 hath made thee a tame snake, and say this to her: that if she love me, I charge her to love thee: if she will not, I will never have her, unless thou entreat for her. If you be a true lover, hence, and not a word, for here comes more company.   [*Exit* Silvius

Enter Oliver

Oliver
75 Good morrow, fair ones. Pray you, if you know,
Where in the purlieus of this forest stands
A sheepcote fenc'd about with olive-trees?

76   *purlieus* : outskirts.

Celia
West of this place, down in the neighbour bottom:
The rank of osiers by the murmuring stream

78   *neighbour bottom* : next valley
79   *osiers* : willow trees.
80   *Left* : left behind.

80 Left on your right hand brings you to the place.

But at this hour the house doth keep itself;
There's none within.
   Oliver
If that an eye may profit by a tongue,
Then should I know you by description;
85 Such garments, and such years: 'The boy is fair,
Of female favour, and bestows himself
Like a ripe sister: the woman low,
And browner than her brother.' Are not you
The owner of the house I did inquire for?
   Celia
90 It is no boast, being ask'd, to say, we are.
   Oliver
Orlando doth commend him to you both,
And to that youth he calls his Rosalind
He sends this bloody napkin. Are you he?
   Rosalind
I am: what must we understand by this?
   Oliver
95 Some of my shame; if you will know of me
What man I am, and how, and why, and where
This handkerchief was stain'd.
   Celia   I pray you, tell it.
   Oliver
When last the young Orlando parted from you
He left a promise to return again
100 Within an hour; and, pacing through the forest,
Chewing the food of sweet and bitter fancy,
Lo, what befell! he threw his eye aside,
And mark what object did present itself:
Under an oak, whose boughs were moss'd with age,
105 And high top bald with dry antiquity,
A wretched ragged man, o'ergrown with hair,
Lay sleeping on his back: about his neck
A green and gilded snake had wreath'd itself,

---

83   If my eyes can recognize you from
what I have been told.

86   *bestows*: behaves.
87   *ripe*: elder.
      low: small.

93   *napkin*: handkerchief.

95   *know of*: learn from.

101   *sweet and bitter fancy*: his thoughts
were sweet because they were about
Rosalind, and bitter because he was
not with her.
102   *befell*: happened.
      threw his eye: glanced.

109 *nimble in threats* : waving about
threateningly.

112 *indented* : zigzag.

114 *drawn dry* : sucked dry her cubs.

116 *When that* : until.

118 *as dead* : as if it were dead.

122 *render him* : describe him as.

127 *purpos'd* : intended to.
128 *kindness* : generosity.
129 *occasion* : cause.

131 *hurtling* : tumult.

135 *'Twas . . . not I* : I was that man,
but now I am not the same man that
I used to be.

Who with her head, nimble in threats, approach'd
110 The opening of his mouth; but suddenly,
Seeing Orlando, it unlink'd itself,
And with indented glides did slip away
Into a bush; under which bush's shade
A lioness, with udders all drawn dry,
115 Lay couching, head on ground, with catlike watch,
When that the sleeping man should stir; for 'tis
The royal disposition of that beast
To prey on nothing that doth seem as dead.
This seen, Orlando did approach the man,
120 And found it was his brother, his elder brother.
            Celia
O I have heard him speak of that same brother;
And he did render him the most unnatural
That liv'd 'mongst men.
            Oliver   And well he might so do,
For well I know he was unnatural.
            Rosalind
125 But, to Orlando: did he leave him there,
Food to the suck'd and hungry lioness?
            Oliver
Twice did he turn his back and purpos'd so:
But kindness, nobler ever than revenge,
And nature, stronger than his just occasion,
130 Made him give battle to the lioness,
Who quickly fell before him: in which hurtling
From miserable slumber I awak'd.
            Celia
Are you his brother?
            Rosalind   Was't you he rescu'd?
            Celia
Was't you that did so oft contrive to kill him?
            Oliver
135 'Twas I; but 'tis not I. I do not shame
To tell you what I was, since my conversion
So sweetly tastes, being the thing I am.
            Rosalind
But, for the bloody napkin?
            Oliver   By and by.

140   *our recountments* : the stories we had
          to tell.
141   *As* : such as.

143   *array* : clothing.

150   *Brief* : in a few words.
          recover'd : restored.
151   *small space* : short time.
          as I am : although I am.

When from the first to last, betwixt us two,
140 Tears our recountments had most kindly bath'd,
As how I came into that desert place,
In brief, he led me to the gentle duke,
Who gave me fresh array and entertainment,
Committing me unto my brother's love;
145 Who led me instantly unto his cave,
There stripp'd himself; and here, upon his arm
The lioness had torn some flesh away,
Which all this while had bled; and now he fainted,
And cried, in fainting, upon Rosalind.
150 Brief, I recover'd him, bound up his wound;
And, after some small space, being strong at heart,
He sent me hither, stranger as I am,
To tell this story, that you might excuse
His broken promise; and to give this napkin,
155 Dyed in his blood, unto the shepherd youth
That he in sport doth call his Rosalind.
                                        [*Rosalind faints*

Celia
Why, how now, Ganymede! sweet Ganymede!
Oliver
Many will swoon when they do look on blood.
Celia
There is more in it. Cousin! Ganymede!
Oliver
160 Look, he recovers.
Rosalind
I would I were at home.
Celia
We'll lead you thither.
I pray you, will you take him by the arm?
Oliver
Be of good cheer, youth. You a man! You lack a
165 man's heart.
Rosalind
I do so, I confess it. Ah, sirrah! a body would
think this was well counterfeited. I pray you, tell
your brother how well I counterfeited. Heigh-ho!

167   *counterfeited* : imitated.

Oliver

This was not counterfeit: there is too great testi-
mony in your complexion that it was a passion of
earnest.

Rosalind

Counterfeit, I assure you.

Oliver

Well then, take a good heart and counterfeit to be
a man.

Rosalind

So I do; but, i' faith, I should have been a woman
by right.

Celia

Come; you look paler and paler: pray you, draw
homewards. Good sir, go with us.

Oliver

That will I, for I must bear answer back how you
excuse my brother, Rosalind.

Rosalind

I shall devise something. But, I pray you, commend
my counterfeiting to him. Will you go?   [*Exeunt*

170-1 *passion of earnest :* real emotion.

170

75

177 *draw :* withdraw.

180

181 *devise :* think of.

Act 5

Act 5   Scene 1

Two fools argue about which of them shall marry Audrey. One fool is Touchstone, the professional comedian, and the other is the simple country lad, William. Naturally, Touchstone is the winner.

8   *no interest in me :* no legal claim on me.

10   *clown :* idiot.
11   *troth :* faith.
12   *be flouting :* have a laugh.
     hold : restrain ourselves.
13   *even :* evening.

14   *God ye :* God give you.

16   *Cover thy head :* put your hat on.
17   *prithee :* I pray you.

Scene 1 *The Forest of Arden*

Enter Touchstone *and* Audrey

Touchstone

We shall find a time, Audrey: patience, gentle Audrey.

Audrey

Faith, the priest was good enough, for all the old gentleman's saying.

Touchstone

5 A most wicked Sir Oliver, Audrey; a most vile Martext. But, Audrey, there is a youth here in the forest lays claim to you.

Audrey

Ay, I know who 'tis: he hath no interest in me in the world. Here comes the man you mean.

Enter William

Touchstone

10 It is meat and drink to me to see a clown. By my troth, we that have good wits have much to answer for: we shall be flouting; we cannot hold.

William

Good even, Audrey.

Audrey

God ye good even, William.

William

15 And good even to you, sir.

Touchstone

Good even, gentle friend. Cover thy head, cover thy head; nay, prithee, be covered. How old are you, friend?

William

Five-and-twenty, sir.

Touchstone

20 A ripe age. Is thy name William?

William

William, sir.

Touchstone

A fair name. Wast born i' the forest here?

William

Ay, sir, I thank God.

Touchstone

'Thank God;' a good answer. Art rich?

William

25 Faith, sir, so-so.

Touchstone

'So-so,' is good, very good, very excellent good: and yet it is not; it is but so-so. Art thou wise?

William

Ay, sir, I have a pretty wit.

Touchstone

Why, thou sayest well. I do now remember a say-
30 ing, 'The fool doth think he is wise, but the wise man knows himself to be a fool.' The heathen philosopher, when he had a desire to eat a grape, would open his lips when he put it into his mouth; meaning thereby that grapes were made to eat and
35 lips to open. You do love this maid?

William

I do, sir.

Touchstone

Give me your hand. Art thou learned?

William

No, sir.

Touchstone

Then learn this of me: to have, is to have; for it is
40 a figure in rhetoric, that drink, being poured out of a cup into a glass, by filling the one doth empty the other; for all your writers do consent that *ipse* is he: now, you are not *ipse*, for I am he.

William

Which he, sir?

Touchstone

45 He, sir, that must marry this woman. Therefore, you clown, abandon—which is in the vulgar, leave—the society—which in the boorish is,

---

25   *so-so :* moderately.

31–5   *The heathen . . . to open.* Touch-stone does not refer to any particular philosopher. Probably William is standing open-mouthed with wonder at the learned man.

37   *learned :* educated.

40   *a figure in rhetoric :* a figure of speech.

42   *consent :* agree.
ipse : Latin for 'he himself'; Touchstone proceeds as though he were an old-fashioned teacher of Latin translation.

46   *the vulgar :* the native language (the vulgar tongue of England is English); but the word can also mean 'boorish' or 'common'.

company—of this female—which in the common
is, woman; which together is, abandon the society
50 of this female, or, clown, thou perishest; or, to thy
better understanding, diest; or, to wit, I kill
thee, make thee away, translate thy life into death,
thy liberty into bondage. I will deal in poison with
thee, or in bastinado, or in steel; I will bandy with
55 thee in faction; I will o'errun thee with policy;
I will kill thee a hundred and fifty ways: therefore
tremble, and depart.

Audrey
Do, good William.

William
God rest you merry, sir.   [*Exit*

Enter Corin

Corin
60 Our master and mistress seek you: come, away,
away!

Touchstone
Trip, Audrey! trip, Audrey! I attend, I attend.
                                         [*Exeunt*

50-1   *to thy . . . understanding :* so that
    you can understand better.
51   *to wit :* that is to say.

54   *bastinado :* beating with a stick.
        in steel : with a sword.
54-5   *bandy . . . in faction :* hurl insults
    at each other.
55   *policy :* scheming.

Scene 2 *Another part of the forest*

Enter Orlando *and* Oliver

Orlando
Is't possible that on so little acquaintance you
should like her? That, but seeing, you should love
her? And, loving, woo? And, wooing, she should
grant? And will you persever to enjoy her?

Oliver
5 Neither call the giddiness of it in question, the
poverty of her, the small acquaintance, my sudden
wooing, nor her sudden consenting; but say with
me, I love Aliena; say with her, that she loves me;
consent with both, that we may enjoy each other:
10 It shall be to your good; for my father's house and
all the revenue that was old Sir Rowland's, will
I estate upon you, and here live and die a shepherd.

Orlando
You have my consent. Let your wedding be to-
morrow: thither will I invite the duke and all's

Act 5   Scene 2
Oliver tells Orlando that he has fallen
in love with Celia. Rosalind (dressed
as Ganymede) tells Orlando that he
shall marry Rosalind at the same time
as Oliver marries Celia. Silvius and
Phebe appear, and they join Rosalind
and Orlando in a poem about love.
Rosalind promises that, on the next
day, they shall all have their wishes
granted.
2   *but :* only.
4   *persever . . . her :* go on to marry
    her.
5-7   *Neither . . . consenting :* do not
    question the impulsiveness of it, nor
    her poverty, nor the fact that we have
    not known each other very long, nor
    her readiness to consent.
11   *revenue :* income.
12   *estate :* settle.

14   *all's :* all his.

15 contented followers. Go you and prepare Aliena;
for, look you, here comes my Rosalind.

Enter Rosalind

Rosalind
God save you, brother.

Oliver
And you, fair sister.   [*Exit*

Rosalind
O my dear Orlando, how it grieves me to see thee
20 wear thy heart in a scarf.

Orlando
It is my arm.

Rosalind
I thought thy heart had been wounded with the
claws of a lion.

Orlando
Wounded it is, but with the eyes of a lady.

Rosalind
25 Did your brother tell you how I counterfeited to
swoon when he showed me your handkerchief?

Orlando
Ay, and greater wonders than that.

Rosalind
O I know where you are. Nay, 'tis true: there was
never anything so sudden but the fight of two rams,
30 and Caesar's thrasonical brag of 'I came, saw, and
overcame:' for your brother and my sister no sooner
met, but they looked; no sooner looked, but they
loved; no sooner loved, but they sighed; no sooner
sighed, but they asked one another the reason; no
35 sooner knew the reason, but they sought the
remedy: and in these degrees have they made a
pair of stairs to marriage, which they will climb
incontinent, or else be incontinent before marriage.
They are in the very wrath of love, and they will
40 together: clubs cannot part them.

Orlando
They shall be married to-morrow, and I will bid
the duke to the nuptial. But, O how bitter a thing
it is to look into happiness through another man's
eyes. By so much the more shall I to-morrow be at
45 the height of heart-heaviness, by how much I shall
think my brother happy in having what he wishes
for.

---

18   *sister :* Oliver, like Orlando, is pretending that Ganymede is Rosalind.

25   *counterfeited :* pretended.

28   *where you are :* what you mean.

30–1   *Caesar's . . . overcame :* Julius Caesar sent the boastful message 'veni, vidi, vici' (I came, I saw, I overcame) to Rome to announce a victory in 47 B.C. Rosalind describes this boast ('brag') as 'thrasonical' because it is in the manner of Thraso, a soldier in the Latin play *Eunuchus*, by Terence.

36   *degrees :* stages; Rosalind then makes a pun on the meaning 'steps'.

38   *incontinent :* immediately; with a pun on the meaning 'unchaste'.

39   *wrath :* passion.

40   *clubs.* When there were riots in London, citizens used to call for 'Clubs' to separate the fighters.

41   *bid :* invite.

Rosalind
Why then, to-morrow I cannot serve your turn for
Rosalind?

Orlando
50 I can live no longer by thinking.

Rosalind
I will weary you then no longer with idle talking.
Know of me then—for now I speak to some purpose—that I know you are a gentleman of good
conceit. I speak not this that you should bear a
55 good opinion of my knowledge, insomuch I say I
know you are; neither do I labour for a greater
esteem than may in some little measure draw a
belief from you, to do yourself good, and not to
grace me. Believe then, if you please, that I can do
60 strange things. I have, since I was three years old,
conversed with a magician, most profound in his
art and yet not damnable. If you do love Rosalind
so near the heart as your gesture cries it out, when
your brother marries Aliena, shall you marry her.
65 I know into what straits of fortune she is driven;
and it is not impossible to me, if it appear not
inconvenient to you, to set her before your eyes
to-morrow, human as she is, and without any
danger.

Orlando
70 Speakest thou in sober meanings?

Rosalind
By my life, I do; which I tender dearly, though
I say I am a magician. Therefore, put you in your
best array; bid your friends; for if you will be
married to-morrow, you shall; and to Rosalind, if
75 you will. Look, here comes a lover of mine, and a
lover of hers.

Enter Silvius *and* Phebe

Phebe
Youth, you have done me much ungentleness,
To show the letter that I writ to you.

Rosalind
I care not if I have: it is my study
80 To seem despiteful and ungentle to you.
You are there follow'd by a faithful shepherd,
Look upon him, love him; he worships you.

52   *Know of me :* learn from me.

54   *conceit :* understanding.
54-9   I don't say this so that you should
        have a good opinion of *my* intelligence,
        simply because I say that I know you
        are intelligent; nor am I trying to give
        you a better opinion of me than is
        necessary to persuade you to believe in
        me to some extent—and this is for
        your own good, not for my credit ('to
        grace me').
61   *conversed :* associated.
        profound : deeply learned.
62   *not damnable :* not evil; it was
        thought that magic, or witchcraft,
        could involve dealings with the devil,
        which would be 'damnable'.
63   *near the heart :* sincerely.
        gesture : behaviour.
65   *straits :* circumstances.
66-7   *not inconvenient :* not altogether
        wrong (i.e. to practise magic).
68-9   *human . . . danger.* If the spirit of
        Rosalind, or a devil in her form, were
        to appear, then Orlando would be in
        danger of damnation. But he is assured
        that there is no need to worry.
70   *in sober meanings :* in plain truth.
71   *tender :* value.
73   *array :* clothes.
        bid : invite.

79   *study :* intention.
80   *despiteful :* contemptuous.

Phebe
Good shepherd, tell this youth what 'tis to love.
Silvius
It is to be all made of sighs and tears;
85 And so am I for Phebe.
Phebe
And I for Ganymede.
Orlando
And I for Rosalind.
Rosalind
And I for no woman.
Silvius
It is to be all made of faith and service;
90 And so am I for Phebe.
Phebe
And I for Ganymede.
Orlando
And I for Rosalind.
Rosalind
And I for no woman.
Silvius
It is to be all made of fantasy,
95 All made of passion, and all made of wishes;
All adoration, duty, and observance;
All humbleness, all patience, and impatience;
All purity, all trial, all obedience;
And so am I for Phebe.
Phebe
100 And so am I for Ganymede.
Orlando
And so am I for Rosalind.
Rosalind
And so am I for no woman.
Phebe
[*To* Rosalind] If this be so, why blame you me to
love you?
Silvius
105 [*To* Phebe] If this be so, why blame you me to love
you?
Orlando
If this be so, why blame you me to love you?

94   *fantasy :* imagination.

96   *observance :* respect.

98   *trial :* endurance.

Rosalind
Who do you speak to, 'Why blame you me to love you?'

Orlando
110 To her that is not here, nor doth not hear.

Rosalind
Pray you, no more of this: 'tis like the howling of Irish wolves against the moon. [*To* Silvius] I will help you, if I can: [*To* Phebe] I would love you, if I could. To-morrow meet me all together. [*To*
115 Phebe] I will marry you, if ever I marry woman, and I'll be married to-morrow: [*To* Orlando] I will satisfy you, if ever I satisfied man, and you shall be married to-morrow: [*To* Silvius] I will content you, if what pleases you contents you, and you shall be
120 married to-morrow. [*To* Orlando] As you love Rosalind, meet: [*To* Silvius] As you love Phebe, meet: and as I love no woman, I'll meet. So, fare you well: I have left you commands.

Silvius
I'll not fail, if I live.

Phebe
125 Nor I.

Orlando
Nor I.   [*Exeunt*

112   *against :* at.

Act 5   Scene 3

This short scene marks the passage of time, separating the scene of Rosalind's promises from the scene in which they are fulfilled.

Scene 3 *Another part of the forest*

Enter Touchstone *and* Audrey

Touchstone
To-morrow is the joyful day, Audrey; to-morrow will we be married.

Audrey
I do desire it with all my heart, and I hope it is no dishonest desire to desire to be a woman of the
5 world. Here come two of the banished duke's pages.

Enter two Pages

First Page
Well met, honest gentleman.

4   *dishonest :* immodest.
4-5   *woman of the world :* married woman.

7   *troth* : faith.

8   *for you* : ready to satisfy you.
    sit i' the middle. There was a rhyme:
    Hey diddle, diddle,
    Fool in the middle.
9   *hawking* : clearing the throat.

12   *in a tune* : together.

Song : For music see p. 100.

17   *ring-time* : time for exchanging
     wedding-rings.

34   *the prime* : all perfections.

Touchstone
By my troth, well met. Come, sit, sit, and a song.
Second Page
We are for you: sit i' the middle.
First Page
Shall we clap into 't roundly, without hawking or
10   spitting, or saying we are hoarse, which are the only
prologues to a bad voice?
Second Page
I' faith, i' faith; and both in a tune, like two gipsies
on a horse.

Song

It was a lover and his lass,
15   *With a hey, and a ho, and a hey nonino,*
That o'er the green corn-field did pass,
    In the spring time, the only pretty ring-time,
When birds do sing, hey ding a ding, ding.
Sweet lovers love the spring.

20   *Between the acres of the rye,*
    With a hey, and a ho, and a hey nonino,
These pretty country folks would lie,
    In the spring time, the only pretty ring-time,
When birds do sing, hey ding a ding, ding.
25   *Sweet lovers love the spring.*

This carol they began that hour,
    With a hey, and a ho, and a hey nonino,
How that a life was but a flower,
    In the spring time, the only pretty ring-time,
30   *When birds do sing, hey ding a ding, ding.*
Sweet lovers love the spring.

And therefore take the present time,
    With a hey, and a ho, and a hey nonino,
For love is crowned with the prime,
35   *In the spring time, the only pretty ring-time,*
When birds do sing, hey ding a ding, ding.
Sweet lovers love the spring.

39   *ditty* : words.
39-40   *the note . . . untuneable* : I did not
        like the tune.

41   *kept time* : i.e. in the singing.

Act 5   Scene 4

All the lovers meet in the Forest.
Rosalind reminds them of their
promises, and then disappears. While
she is away, Touchstone amuses the
other characters—and gives Rosalind
time to exchange Ganymede's clothes
for her own. There is a poetic
wedding, celebrated by Hymen, the
classical god of marriage. Jaques de
Boys, a character we have not seen
before, comes to tell Duke Senior
that his brother has repented and
given up the dukedom. Duke Senior
and all the other characters except
Jaques decide to return to the court.

4   They fear that their hopes may be
        unfounded, and they know that they
        are afraid.

5   *Whiles . . . urg'd* : whilst our agree-
        ment is stated again.

Touchstone

Truly, young gentlemen, though there was no
great matter in the ditty, yet the note was very
40 untuneable.
    First Page
You are deceived, sir : we kept time ; we lost not
our time.
    Touchstone
By my troth, yes ; I count it but time lost to hear
such a foolish song. God be wi' you ; and God mend
45 your voices ! Come, Audrey.   [*Exeunt*

Scene 4 *Another part of the forest*

        Enter Duke Senior, Amiens, Jaques,
            Orlando, Oliver, *and* Celia
    Duke Senior
Dost thou believe, Orlando, that the boy
Can do all this that he hath promised ?
    Orlando
I sometimes do believe, and sometimes do not ;
As those that fear they hope, and know they fear.

        Enter Rosalind, Silvius, *and* Phebe
    Rosalind
5 Patience once more, whiles our compact is urg'd.
[*To the* Duke] You say, if I bring in your Rosalind,
You will bestow her on Orlando here ?
    Duke Senior
That would I, had I kingdoms to give with her.
    Rosalind
[*To* Orlando] And you say, you will have her when
    I bring her ?
    Orlando
10 That would I, were I of all kingdoms king.
    Rosalind
[*To* Phebe] You say, you'll marry me, if I be
    willing ?
    Phebe
That will I, should I die the hour after.
    Rosalind
But if you do refuse to marry me,
You'll give yourself to this most faithful shepherd ?

Phebe

15 So is the bargain.

Rosalind

[*To* Silvius] You say, that you'll have Phebe, if
she will?

Silvius

Though to have her and death were both one
thing.

Rosalind

I have promis'd to make all this matter even.
Keep you your word, O duke, to give your daughter;
20 You yours, Orlando, to receive his daughter;
Keep you your word, Phebe, that you'll marry me,
Or else, refusing me, to wed this shepherd;
Keep your word, Silvius, that you'll marry her,
If she refuse me: and from hence I go,
25 To make these doubts all even.

[*Exeunt* Rosalind *and* Celia

Duke Senior

I do remember in this shepherd boy
Some lively touches of my daughter's favour.

Orlando

My lord, the first time that I ever saw him,
Methought he was a brother to your daughter;
30 But, my good lord, this boy is forest-born,
And hath been tutor'd in the rudiments
Of many desperate studies by his uncle,
Whom he reports to be a great magician,
Obscured in the circle of this forest.

Enter Touchstone *and* Audrey

Jaques

35 There is, sure, another flood toward, and these
couples are coming to the ark. Here comes a pair
of very strange beasts, which in all tongues are
called fools.

Touchstone

Salutation and greeting to you all!

Jaques

40 Good my lord, bid him welcome. This is the motley-
minded gentleman that I have so often met in the
forest: he hath been a courtier, he swears.

18 *to make . . . even :* solve all these
problems.

27 *lively :* life-like.
favour : appearance.

32 *desperate :* dangerous.

34 *Obscured :* hidden.
circle. A magician had to draw a
circle round himself, so that he could
not be harmed by any evil spirits that
came in response to his conjuring.

35 *toward :* coming.

40 *motley-minded :* having the mind of a
fool (as well as the costume).

Touchstone
If any man doubt that, let him put me to my
purgation. I have trod a measure; I have flattered
45 a lady; I have been politic with my friend, smooth
with mine enemy; I have undone three tailors;
I have had four quarrels, and like to have fought
one.

Jaques
And how was that ta'en up?

Touchstone
50 Faith, we met, and found the quarrel was upon the
seventh cause.

Jaques
How seventh cause? Good my lord, like this fellow.

Duke Senior
I like him very well.

Touchstone
God 'ild you, sir; I desire you of the like. I press in
55 here, sir, amongst the rest of the country copulatives, to swear, and to forswear, according as
marriage binds and blood breaks. A poor virgin,
sir, an ill-favoured thing, sir, but mine own: a poor
humour of mine, sir, to take that that no man else
60 will. Rich honesty dwells like a miser, sir, in a poor
house, as your pearl in your foul oyster.

Duke Senior
By my faith, he is very swift and sententious.

Touchstone
According to the fool's bolt, sir, and such dulcet
diseases.

Jaques
65 But, for the seventh cause; how did you find the
quarrel on the seventh cause?

Touchstone
Upon a lie seven times removed—bear your body
more seeming, Audrey—as thus, sir. I did dislike
the cut of a certain courtier's beard: he sent me
70 word, if I said his beard was not cut well, he was in
the mind it was: this is called the Retort Courteous.
If I sent him word again, it was not well cut, he
would send me word, he cut it to please himself:
this is called the Quip Modest. If again, it was not

44   *purgation* : proof.
      trod a measure : danced a stately
dance.
45   *politic* : cunning.
      smooth : polite.
46   *undone* : ruined (by not paying their
bills).
47   *like to have fought* : almost had to
fight.
49   *ta'en up* : settled.

51   *the seventh cause* : Touchstone
explains this in lines 67–101.

54   *God 'ild you* : may God reward you.
      I . . . like : I hope you continue to
like me.
55   *country copulatives* : country folk
who are going to be married.
57   As marriage binds us together, and
as my lust ('blood') forces me to break
the bonds.
58   *ill-favoured* : ugly.
59   *humour* : whim.
60   *Rich honesty* : Precious chastity.
62   *swift* : quick-witted.
      sententious : full of epigrams.
63   *fool's bolt*. There is a proverb,
'A fool's bolt [arrow] is soon shot',
meaning that a fool speaks before he
thinks.
63–4 *dulcet diseases* : pleasant weak-
nesses; Touchstone is very humble
about his profession when he talks to
the duke.
65   *find* : solve.
68   *seeming* : decently.

70–1 *was in the mind* : thought that.

74   *Quip* : retort.

75   *disabled my judgement* : said I wasn't fit to judge.

80   *Circumstantial* : depending on the circumstances.

85   *measured swords.* Before a duel, the opponents had to make sure that their swords were of equal length; in the case Touchstone describes, the measuring was a mere formality, since no fight took place.

86   *nominate* : name.

88   *in print* : according to the book of rules.

97   *justices* : magistrates.
      take up : settle.

98-9   *thought but of* : simply thought of.

100   *swore brothers* : swore to behave like brothers.

104   *stalking-horse* : a horse which the hunter hides behind when stalking his prey.

105   *presentation of that* : appearance of foolishness.

105sd   *Hymen* : the Roman god of marriage. When this play is performed, the director must decide whether to have the part of Hymen acted by one of the other characters in the play (under Rosalind's instructions); the alternative is to allow the god himself to appear, thus suggesting that there is real magic in this happy ending. See Introduction, p. xxii.

---

75   well cut, he disabled my judgement: this is called the Reply Churlish. If again, it was not well cut, he would answer, I spake not true: this is called the Reproof Valiant: if again, it was not well cut, he would say, I lie: this is called the Countercheck

80   Quarrelsome: and so to the Lie Circumstantial, and the Lie Direct.

Jaques
And how oft did you say his beard was not well cut?

Touchstone
I durst go no further than the Lie Circumstantial, nor he durst not give me the Lie Direct; and so we

85   measured swords and parted.

Jaques
Can you nominate in order now the degrees of the lie?

Touchstone
O sir, we quarrel in print; by the book, as you have books for good manners: I will name you the

90   degrees. The first, the Retort Courteous; the second, the Quip Modest; the third, the Reply Churlish; the fourth, the Reproof Valiant; the fifth, the Countercheck Quarrelsome; the sixth, the Lie with Circumstance; the seventh, the Lie Direct. All

95   these you may avoid but the Lie Direct; and you may avoid that too, with an 'if.' I knew when seven justices could not take up a quarrel; but when the parties were met themselves, one of them thought but of an 'if,' as 'If you said so, then I said so;' and

100   they shook hands and swore brothers. Your 'if' is the only peace-maker; much virtue in 'if.'

Jaques
Is not this a rare fellow, my lord? he's as good at any thing, and yet a fool.

Duke Senior
He uses his folly like a stalking-horse, and under

105   the presentation of that he shoots his wit.

Enter Hymen, *leading* Rosalind *in woman's clothes, and* Celia. *Music*

Hymen
Then is there mirth in heaven,

107   *made even :* smoothed out.
108   *Atone :* harmonize.

113   *Whose :* i.e. Rosalind's; many love
       poems of this period speak of the
       interchange of hearts—so that the
       man's heart is in the woman's body,
       and vice versa.

123   *bar :* forbid.

127   *Hymen's bands :* bonds of marriage.
128   If, now that you know the truth, you
       are still contented (with your partners).

131   *accord :* consent.

133   *sure together :* as suitable for one
       another.

137   When you understand, you will not
       be so surprised.

When earthly things made even
      Atone together.
Good duke, receive thy daughter;
110   Hymen from heaven brought her;
      Yea, brought her hither,
That thou mightst join her hand with his,
      Whose heart within his bosom is.

Rosalind
[*To* Duke Senior] To you I give myself, for I am
yours.
115   [*To* Orlando] To you I give myself, for I am yours.
      Duke Senior
If there be truth in sight, you are my daughter.
      Orlando
If there be truth in sight, you are my Rosalind.
      Phebe
If sight and shape be true,
Why then, my love adieu!
      Rosalind
120   [*To* Duke Senior] I'll have no father, if you be
not he.
[*To* Orlando] I'll have no husband, if you be not he:
[*To* Phebe] Nor ne'er wed woman, if you be not
she.
      Hymen
Peace, ho! I bar confusion:
'Tis I must make conclusion
125   Of these most strange events:
Here's eight that must take hands
To join in Hymen's bands,
      If truth holds true contents.
[*To* Orlando *and* Rosalind] You and you no
      cross shall part:
130   [*To* Oliver *and* Celia] You and you are heart
      in heart:
[*To* Phebe] You to his love must accord,
Or have a woman to your lord:
[*To* Touchstone *and* Audrey] You and you are
      sure together,
As the winter to foul weather.
135   Whiles a wedlock hymn we sing,
Feed yourselves with questioning,
That reason wonder may diminish,
How thus we met, and these things finish.

Song

139   *Juno* : queen of the classical gods,
  and goddess of marriage.
140   *board* : table.

140
Wedding is great Juno's crown :
  O blessed bond of board and bed!
'Tis Hymen peoples every town ;
  High wedlock then be honoured.
Honour, high honour, and renown,
To Hymen, god of every town!

Duke Senior
145 O my dear niece! welcome thou art to me :
   Even daughter, welcome in no less degree.
  Phebe
   [*To* Silvius] I will not eat my word, now thou art
    mine ;
   Thy faith my fancy to thee doth combine.

146   *Even daughter* : as though you
  were my daughter.

Enter Jaques de Boys

Jaques de Boys
   Let me have audience for a word or two :
150 I am the second son of old Sir Rowland,
   That bring these tidings to this fair assembly.
   Duke Frederick, hearing how that every day
   Men of great worth resorted to this forest,
   Address'd a mighty power, which were on foot
155 In his own conduct, purposely to take
   His brother here and put him to the sword :
   And to the skirts of this wild wood he came,
   Where, meeting with an old religious man,
   After some question with him, was converted
160 Both from his enterprise and from the world ;
   His crown bequeathing to his banish'd brother,
   And all their lands restor'd to them again
   That were with him exil'd. This to be true,
   I do engage my life.
  Duke Senior   Welcome, young man ;
165 Thou offer'st fairly to thy brothers' wedding :
   To one, his lands withheld ; and to the other
   A land itself at large, a potent dukedom.
   First, in this forest, let us do those ends
   That here were well begun and well begot ;

148   Your faithfulness binds my love
  to you.

151   *tidings* : news.

153   *great worth* : high rank.
154   *Address'd* : made ready.
    power : army.
154-5 *which . . . conduct* : which had
  already set out under his own
  leadership.
155   *purposely* : with the intention.
156   *to the sword* : to death.
157   *skirts* : outskirts.
158   *religious man* : hermit.
159   *question* : conversation.
160   *the world* : worldly things.

164   *engage* : pledge.

165   *offer'st fairly* : bring a handsome
  present.
166   *To one . . . withheld* : to Oliver,
  the lands which Duke Frederick had
  taken from him (in *Act 2*, Scene 2).
167   *at large* : complete.
    potent : mighty.
168   *do those ends* : finish those things.

170	*every* : each one.
171	*shrewd* : sharp.
173	*According . . . states* : in proportion to their ranks.
174	*new-fall'n* : recent.
177	*measure . . . joy* : cup full of happiness; Duke Senior may be referring to Psalm 23:5, 'my cup runneth over'.
	to . . . fall : join in the dancing.
178	*Sir . . . patience.* This is addressed to Duke Senior; Jaques excuses himself before speaking to Jaques de Boys.
180	*pompous* : full of pomp.
182	*out of* : from.
	convertites : religious converts.
189	*wrangling* : quarrelling.
189–90	Your marriage is like a ship that carries food for no more than two months.
193	*would have* : want to know.

170 And after, every of this happy number
That have endur'd shrewd days and nights with us,
Shall share the good of our returned fortune,
According to the measure of their states.
Meantime, forget this new-fall'n dignity,
175 And fall into our rustic revelry.
Play, music! and you, brides and bridegrooms all,
With measure heap'd in joy, to the measures fall.
      Jaques
Sir, by your patience. If I heard you rightly,
The duke hath put on a religious life,
180 And thrown into neglect the pompous court?
      Jaques de Boys
He hath.
      Jaques
To him will I: out of these convertites
There is much matter to be heard and learn'd.
[*To* Duke Senior] You to your former honour I
      bequeath;
185 Your patience and your virtue well deserves it:
[*To* Orlando] You to a love that your true faith doth
      merit:
[*To* Oliver] You to your land, and love, and great
      allies:
[*To* Silvius] You to a long and well-deserved bed:
[*To* Touchstone] And you to wrangling; for thy
      loving voyage
190 Is but for two months victual'd. So, to your
      pleasures:
I am for other than for dancing measures.
      Duke Senior
Stay, Jaques, stay.
      Jaques
To see no pastime, I: what you would have
I'll stay to know at your abandon'd cave.   [*Exit*
      Duke Senior
195 Proceed, proceed: we will begin these rites,
As we do trust they'll end, in true delights.
      [*A dance. Exeunt all except* Rosalind

197   *the lady the epilogue :* one of the female characters speak the epilogue.

199–200   *good wine . . . bush :* if a thing is good, it needs no advertising. This is a proverb, referring to the branches which a wine-merchant hung outside his shop for an advertisement.

203   *case :* situation; Rosalind puns on another meaning, 'costume'.

204   *insinuate :* plead.

205   *furnished :* dressed.

206   *become :* suit.

207   *conjure :* charm (as though Rosalind were the magician she claimed to be in 5, 2, 59).

211   *simpering :* smiling.

213   *If I were a woman.* Remember that boy actors played female roles at this time.

215   *liked :* pleased.

216   *defied :* disliked.

218–19   *bid me farewell :* i.e. by clapping.

Rosalind

It is not the fashion to see the lady the epilogue;
but it is no more unhandsome than to see the lord
the prologue. If it be true that good wine needs no
200 bush, 'tis true that a good play needs no epilogue;
yet to good wine they do use good bushes, and good
plays prove the better by the help of good epilogues.
What a case am I in then, that am neither a good
epilogue, nor cannot insinuate with you in the
205 behalf of a good play! I am not furnished like a
beggar, therefore to beg will not become me: my
way is, to conjure you; and I'll begin with the
women. I charge you, O women, for the love you
bear to men, to like as much of this play as please
210 you: and I charge you, O men, for the love you bear
to women—as I perceive by your simpering none
of you hate them—that between you and the
women, the play may please. If I were a woman,
I would kiss as many of you as had beards that
215 pleased me, complexions that liked me, and breaths
that I defied not; and, I am sure, as many as have
good beards, or good faces, or sweet breaths, will,
for my kind offer, when I make curtsy, bid me
farewell.   [*Exit*

IT WAS A LOVER AND HIS LASS

'It was a lover and his lass' (*Act 5*, Scene 3)

A musical setting for this attractive lyric is to be found in Thomas Morley's *First Book of Airs*, published in 1600.

o'er   the   green   corn - fields   did   pass,
pret - ty   coun - try   fools   would   lie,
that   a   life   was   but   a   flower,
love   is   crown - ed   with   the   prime,
} In   Spring   time,   in

Spring   time,   in   Spring   time,   the   on - ly   pret - ty   ring - time, When

birds   do   sing   hey   ding a ding a ding,   hey   ding a ding a ding,   hey

Classwork and Examinations

The works of Shakespeare are studied all over the world, and this classroom edition is being used in many different countries. Teaching methods vary from school to school, and there are many different ways of examining a student's work. Some teachers and examiners expect detailed knowledge of Shakespeare's text; others ask for imaginative involvement with his characters and their situations; and there are some teachers who want their students to share in the theatrical experience of directing and performing a play. Most people use a variety of methods. This section of the book offers a few suggestions for approaches to *As You Like It* which could be used in schools and colleges to help with students' understanding and *enjoyment* of the play.

    A Discussion
    B Character Study
    C Activities
    D Context Questions
    E Comprehension Questions
    F Essays
    G Projects

A Discussion

Talking about the play—about the issues it raises and the characters who are involved—is one of the most rewarding and pleasurable aspects of the study of Shakespeare. It makes sense to discuss each scene as it is read, sharing impressions—and perhaps correcting misapprehensions. It can be useful to compare aspects of this play with other fictions—plays, novels, films—or with modern life.

Suggestions

A1 When Rosalind and Celia are invited to watch the wrestling in *Act 1*, Scene 2, Touchstone observes 'it is the first time that ever I heard breaking of ribs was sport for ladies' (127–9). Do you agree with his attitude?

A2 Celia is surprised when Rosalind declares her feelings for Orlando: 'is it possible, on such a sudden, you should fall into such a liking?' (*1*, 3, 25–6). Do *you* believe in love at first sight?

A3 In the forest of Arden, Duke Senior addresses his followers:

> shall we go and kill us venison?
> And yet it irks me the poor dappled fools,
> Being native burghers of this desert city,
> Should, in their own confines, with forked heads,
> Have their round haunches gor'd.
>
> (*2*, 1, 21–5)

How do you react to this speech?

A4 Duke Senior asserts that the simple life in the Forest of Arden is 'more sweet Than that of painted pomp' (*2*, 1, 2–3). What is your idea of the Good Life?

A5 By 'courtesy of nations' (*1*, 1, 46) the eldest son inherits all. Is this fair?

A6 Would anything be gained—or lost—by staging this play in modern dress?

A7 Discuss the social functions of satire in the light of Jaques' comments (*2*, 7, 45–87). Is there any modern equivalent for the court fool?

B   Character Study

Shakespeare is famous for his creation of characters who seem like real people. We can judge their actions and we can try to understand their thoughts and feelings—just as we criticize and try to understand the people we know. As the play progresses, we learn to like or dislike, love or hate, them—just as though they lived in *our* world.

Characters can be studied *from the outside*, by observing what they do, and listening sensitively to what they say. This is the scholar's method: the scholar—or any reader—has access to the whole play, and can see the function of every character within the whole scheme of that play.

Another approach works *from the inside*, taking a single character and looking at the action and the other characters from his/her point of view. This is an actor's technique when creating a character—who can have only a partial view of what is going on—for performance; and it asks for a student's inventive imagination. The two methods—both useful in different ways—are really complementary to each other.

Suggestions

a) from 'outside' the character

B1 Compare the characters of
a) Rosalind and Celia
b) Duke Senior and Duke Frederick
c) Oliver and Orlando

B2 Discuss the characters and dramatic functions of
a) Jaques
b) Touchstone
c) Adam

B3 Compare Orlando and Silvius as romantic lovers.

B4 Why do you think that Shakespeare introduces the truly rural characters—Corin, Audrey, and William—into this pastoral fantasy?

B5 'Not one of the characters in *As You Like It* is truly credible: their passions are always too extreme.' Do you agree?

b) from 'inside' a character

B6 As Orlando, give an account of your young life, filling in the details of your brother's harsh treatment.

B7 Give full media coverage—newspaper, radio, television—to the wrestling matches in *Act 1*, Scene 2, being very sure to get interviews with Charles, the chief wrestler, and with people who hold strong views about such 'sports'.

B8 Write Adam's memoirs of his service with 'old Sir Rowland'.

B9   All the world's a stage,
And all the men and women merely players.
They have their exits and their entrances,
And one man in his time plays many parts,
His acts being seven ages.

2, 7, 139–143

Jaques proceeds to describe 'the Seven Ages of Man'. Write 'the Seven Ages of Woman'.

B10 Celia gives—*1*, 3, 71–4—a very succinct account of her friendship with Rosalind. Describe the relationship with *your* best friend.

B11 Re-write Orlando's verses—*Act 3*, Scene 2—in a modern idiom.

B12 In Celia's diary describe your observation of Rosalind's love affair with Orlando.

B13 In the character of Audrey, (*a*) tell your parents about Jaques and your woodland 'marriage' in *Act 3*, Scene 3; (*b*) talk to William about your marriage to Jaques which may— or may not—have been 'but for two months victual'd' (*5*, 4, 189).

B14 Write a letter from Phebe to her girlfriend, telling her all about Silvius and your meeting with 'Ganymede'.

B15 In Orlando's diary, confide your feelings after the mock marriage (*Act 4*, Scene 1) with the boy whom you called 'Rosalind'.

B16 The reformed Oliver identifies himself to Rosalind, saying

> I do not shame
> To tell you what I was, since my conversion
> So sweetly tastes, being the thing I am.
>
> *4*, 3, 135–7

In Oliver's diary (or letter to his friend), reveal all the stages in your 'conversion'.

B17 Recount the events of *Act 5*, Scene 4 as seen through the eyes of

    a) Duke Senior   c) Silvius
    b) Orlando   d) Phebe

B18 We are told (*5*, 4, 152–62) how Duke Frederick followed his brother into the Forest of Arden

> Where, meeting with an old religious man,
> After some question with him, [he] was converted.

Write the Duke's story, *either* as an intimate letter to a close friend, *or* for publication as a feature-article: '"Why I renounced the world": thoughts of a ducal drop-out'.

B19 'Where are they now?' Celia, former head girl of Arden High School, writes for the school magazine describing events leading up to the double marriage.

B20 Several Lords followed Duke Senior into the Forest of Arden (where they could 'fleet the time carelessly, as they did in the golden world', *1*, 1, 116–7). As one of these Lords, explain your action to the wife or friends you left at court; describe your life in the Forest and your feelings about your return.

C Activities

These can involve two or more students, preferably working *away from* the desk or study-table and using gesture and position ('body-language') as well as speech. They can help students to develop a sense of drama and the dramatic aspects of Shakespeare's play—which was written to be *performed*, not studied in a classroom.

Suggestions

C1 Act the play—or at least a few scenes of it.

C2 Organize a 'town *versus* country' debate between those who share Duke Senior's views and those who take sides with Touchstone (see *2*, 1, 2–4 *and 2*, 4, 14–15)

> Hath not old custom made this life more sweet
> Than that of painted pomp? Are not these woods
> More free from peril than the envious court?

and

> '. . . now I am in Arden; the more fool I: when I was at home, I was in a better place'.

C3 Produce a holiday brochure or television commercial for Duke's Travel Agency Forest Retreats (perhaps with special discounts for senior citizens).

C4 When it comes, will it come without warning
>   Just as I'm picking my nose?
> Will it knock on my door in the morning,
>   Or tread in the bus on my toes?
> Will it come like a change in the weather?
>   Will its greeting be courteous or rough?
> Will it alter my life altogether?
>   O tell me the truth about love.

(W.H. Auden, Song XII)

Organize a classroom debate to answer Auden's question. How would the question be answered by the different characters in *As You Like It*?

C5 Orlando's verses have been re-written in modern idiom (see B11). Devise a scene in which they are discussed by modern Rosalind and Celia.

D   Context Questions

In written examinations, these questions present you with short passages from the play, and ask you to explain them. They are intended to test your knowledge of the play and your understanding of its words. Usually you have to make a choice of passages: there may be five on the paper, and you are asked to choose three. Be very sure that you know exactly how many passages you must choose. Study the ones offered to you, and select those you feel most certain of. Make your answers accurate and concise—don't waste time writing more than the examiner is asking for.

D1 Good my complexion! Dost thou think though I am caparisoned like a man I have a doublet and hose in my disposition? One inch of delay more is a South Sea of discovery. I prithee tell me who it is, and speak apace.

   (i) Who is the speaker? Who is referred to?
   (ii) Why is the speaker 'caparisoned like a man'? What name does she use when she is appearing as a man?
   (iii) Who comes on to the stage after this speech? What does the speaker offer to do?

D2   He threw his eye aside,
And mark what object did present itself.
Under an old oak, whose boughs were moss'd with age,
And high top bald with dry antiquity,
A wretched ragged man, o'ergrown with hair,
Lay sleeping on his back.

   (i) Who is the speaker? To whom does he speak?
   (ii) Who are the two men referred to in the passage?
   (iii) What happened when the sleeping man awoke? What effect does this story have on one of the hearers?

D3 I remember when I was in love. I broke my sword upon a
stone, and bid him take that for coming a-night to Jane Smile;
and I remember the kissing of her batler, and the cow's dugs
that her pretty chopt hands had milked.

    (i) Who is speaking? To whom is he speaking?
   (ii) Why is the speaker in his present situation?
  (iii) What two persons have reminded the speaker of the time
       when he was in love?

D4 Then but forbear your food a little while,
Whiles, like a doe, I go to find my fawn,
And give it food. There is an old poor man,
Who after me hath many a weary step
Limp'd in pure love.

    (i) Who is compared to the doe, and who is the fawn?
   (ii) Why has the old man accompanied the speaker, and why
       has the speaker made this journey?
  (iii) To whom are these lines addressed? Why are they in this
       place?

D5 But let your fair eyes and gentle wishes go with me to my trial;
wherein if I be foiled, there is but one shamed that was never
gracious; if killed, but one dead that is willing to be so.

    (i) Who is the speaker? Whose are the 'fair eyes and gentle
       wishes'?
   (ii) What is the 'trial' that is mentioned? What is the result of
       this trial?
  (iii) Why is the speaker willing to be dead? How do we know
       that he is in more danger than he suspects?

D6 Neither call the giddiness of it in question, the poverty of her,
the small acquaintance, my sudden wooing, nor her sudden
consenting. But say with me, I love—; say with her, that she
loves me; consent with both, that we may enjoy each other.

    (i) Who is speaking? To whom does he speak?
   (ii) What does he call the woman he loves? What is her real
       name?
  (iii) What does he offer to the person addressed?

D7 And will you, being a man of your breeding, be married under
a bush like a beggar? Get you to church, and have a good
priest that can tell you what marriage is. This fellow will but
join you together as they join wainscot, then one of you will
prove a shrunk panel, and like green timber, warp, warp.

(i) Who is the speaker? To whom does he speak?
(ii) Who is 'This fellow', and who is to be joined in marriage
to the person addressed?
(iii) Why has the person addressed chosen to be married in
this way? Is the marriage expected to last for a long time?

D8 Why would you be so fond to overcome
The bonny prizer of the humorous duke?
Your praise is come too swiftly home before you.
Know you not, master, to some kind of men,
Their graces serve them but as enemies?
No more do yours.

(i) Who is the speaker? Who is his 'master'?
(ii) What is the event he refers to? Who is 'the humorous
duke'?
(iii) Why does the speaker warn the person addressed? What
does this person decide to do?

E Comprehension Questions

These also present passages from the play and ask questions about
them, and again you often have a choice of passages. But the
extracts are much longer than those presented as context questions.
A detailed knowledge of the language of the play is asked for here,
and you must be able to express unusual or archaic phrases in your
own words; you may also be asked to comment critically on the
effectiveness of Shakespeare's language.

E1 *Orlando*
Speak you so gently? Pardon me, I pray you:
I thought that all things had been savage here,
And therefore put I on the countenance
Of stern commandment. But whate'er you are
That in this desert inaccessible,
Under the shade of melancholy boughs,

5

Lose and neglect the creeping hours of time;
If ever you have look'd on better days,
If ever been where bells have knoll'd to church,
If ever sat at any good man's feast,   10
If ever from your eyelids wip'd a tear,
And know what 'tis to pity, and be pitied,
Let gentleness my strong enforcement be:
In the which hope I blush, and hide my sword.

> (i) What is the meaning of 'gently' (line 1); 'countenance'
> (line 4); 'commandment' (line 5); 'enforcement' (line 13).
> (ii) Express in your own words the sense of lines 3–4,
> ('therefore . . . commandment'); line 7, ('Lose . . .
> time'); line 9 ('bells . . . church'); line 13 ('Let . . .
> be').
> (iii) Comment on the style of this passage.
> (iv) How do these lines contrast the life at court with life in
> the country?

E2 *Adam*

                          O my gentle master!
O my sweet master! O you memory
Of old Sir Rowland! why, what make you here?
Why are you virtuous? Why do people love you?
And wherefore are you gentle, strong and valiant?   5
Why would you be so fond to overcome
The bonny prizer of the humorous duke?
Your praise is come too swiftly home before you.
Know you not, master, to some kind of men
Their graces serve them but as enemies?   10
No more do yours: your virtues, gentle master,
Are sanctified and holy traitors to you.
O, what a world is this, when what is comely
Envenoms him that bears it!

> (i) Give the meaning of 'make' (line 3); 'fond' (line 6);
> 'bonny' (line 7); 'humorous' (line 7).
> (ii) Express in your own words the sense of line 10, ('Their
> . . . enemies'); lines 11–12, ('your . . . to you'); lines
> 13–14, ('what . . . bears it').
> (iii) What do these lines show of the character of Adam?
> (iv) How are past and present contrasted in this passage?

E3 *Rosalind*

No, faith proud mistress, hope not after it:
'Tis not your inky brows, your black silk hair,
Your bugle eyeballs, nor your cheek of cream,
That can entame my spirits to your worship.
You foolish shepherd, wherefore do you follow her,   5
Like foggy south, puffing with wind and rain?
You are a thousand times a properer man
Than she a woman: 'tis such fools as you
That make the world full of ill-favour'd children:
'Tis not her glass, but you, that flatters her;   10
And out of you she sees herself more proper
Than any of her lineaments can show her.
But, mistress, know yourself: down on your knees,
And thank heaven, fasting, for a good man's love.

(i) Give the meaning of 'bugle' (line 3); 'entame' (line 4); 'ill-favour'd' (line 9); 'proper' (line 11).
(ii) Express in your own words the sense of line 6, ('Like . . . rain'); lines 11–12, ('out of you . . . her'); 13–14 ('down . . . love').
(iii) How is the character of the speaker expressed in these lines?

F   Essays

These will usually give you a specific topic to discuss, or perhaps a question that must be answered, in writing, *with a reasoned argument*. They *never* want you to tell the story of the play—so don't! Your examiner—or teacher—has read the play, and does not need to be reminded of it. Relevant quotations will always help you to make your points more strongly.

F1   Compare the relationship between Oliver and Orlando with that of Duke Senior and Duke Frederick.

F2   What impressions of life at the court do we gain from Charles and Le Beau?

F3   Show how Rosalind's wit and humour conceal an inner sadness.

F4   By comparing her behaviour towards Orlando at court and in the Forest, show what freedom Rosalind gained by changing her costume.

F5 Describe in detail your reaction to the character of Rosalind.

F6 Do you agree that Celia is completely over-shadowed by Rosalind? How would you describe the character of Celia?

F7 Show how several characters reveal their natures by their comments on Sir Rowland de Boys.

F8 In *As You Like It*, nothing very much happens. What do you consider to be the most important way (or ways) in which Shakespeare compensates for this lack of action?

F9 'Their graces serve them but as enemies': discuss the themes of virtue, and the envy of virtue, in *As You Like It*.

F10 'Touchstone and Jaques are extraneous to the plot but essential to the play.' With reference to *either* Touchstone *or* Jaques, explain this statement. Do you agree with it?

F11 'Both Rosalind and Phebe try to bring their lovers to a better understanding of love; their methods are the same, but the audience must react differently.' Why do you think this might have been said?

F12 'Duke Senior and his followers escape to the Forest of Arden; but this does not mean that they are escapists.' Can you explain this statement?

G Projects

In some schools, students are asked to do more 'free-ranging' work, which takes them outside the text—but which should always be relevant to the play. Such Projects may demand skills other than reading and writing: design and artwork, for instance, may be involved. Sometimes a 'portfolio' of work is assembled over a considerable period of time; and this can be presented to the examiner as part of the student's work for assessment.

The availability of resources will, obviously, do much to determine the nature of the Projects; but this is something that only the local teachers will understand. However, there is always help to be found in libraries, museums, and art galleries.

Suggestions

G1 The Good Life.

G2 The court fool.

G3 Great actresses in *As You Like It*.

G4 Rural Retreats.

G5 Pastoral Literature.

Background

England c. 1599

When Shakespeare was writing *As You Like It*, most people believed that the sun went round the earth. They were taught that this was a divinely ordered scheme of things, and that—in England—God had instituted a Church and ordained a Monarchy for the right government of the land and the populace.

'The past is a foreign country; they do things differently there.'

L.P. Hartley

Government

For most of Shakespeare's life, the reigning monarch of England was Queen Elizabeth I. With her counsellors and ministers, she governed the nation (population about five million) from London, although not more than half a million people inhabited the capital city. In the rest of the country, law and order were maintained by the land-owners and enforced by their deputies. The average man had no vote—and his wife had no rights at all.

Religion

At this time, England was a Christian country. All children were baptized, soon after they were born, into the Church of England; they were taught the essentials of the Christian faith, and instructed in their duty to God and to humankind.

Marriages were performed, and funerals conducted, only by the licensed clergy and in accordance with the Church's rites and ceremonies. Attendance at divine service was compulsory; absences (without good—medical—reason) could be punished by fines. By such means, the authorities were able to keep some check on the populace—recording births, marriages, and deaths; being alert to any religious nonconformity, which could be politically dangerous; and ensuring a minimum of orthodox instruction through the official 'Homilies' which were regularly preached from the pulpits of all parish churches throughout the realm.

Following Henry VIII's break away from the Church of Rome, all people in England were able to hear the church services *in their own language*. The Book of Common Prayer was used in every church, and an English translation of the Bible was read aloud in public. The Christian religion had never been so well taught before!

Education

School education reinforced the Church's teaching. From the age of four, boys might attend the 'petty school' (French '*petite école*') to learn the rudiments of reading and writing along with a few prayers; some schools also included work with numbers. At the age of seven, the boy was ready for the grammar school (if his father was willing and able to pay the fees).

Here, a thorough grounding in Latin grammar was followed by translation work and the study of Roman authors, paying attention as much to style as to matter. The arts of fine writing were thus inculcated from early youth.

A very few students proceeded to university; these were either clever scholarship boys, or else the sons of noblemen. Girls stayed at home, and acquired domestic and social skills—cooking, sewing, perhaps even music. The lucky ones might learn to read and write.

Language

At the start of the sixteenth century the English had a very poor opinion of their own language: there was little serious writing in English, and hardly any literature. Latin was the language of international scholarship, and Englishmen admired the eloquence of the Romans. They made many translations, and in this way they extended the resources of their own language, increasing its vocabulary and stretching its grammatical structures. French, Italian, and Spanish works were also translated, and for the first time, there were English versions of the Bible.

By the end of the century, English was a language to be proud of: it was rich in synonyms, capable of infinite variety and subtlety, and ready for all kinds of word-play—especially the *puns*, for which Shakespeare's English is renowned.

Drama

The great art-form of the Elizabethan and Jacobean age was its drama. The Elizabethans inherited a tradition of play-acting from the Middle Ages, and they reinforced this by reading and translating the Roman playwrights. At the beginning of the sixteenth century, plays were performed by groups of actors, all-male companies (boys acted the female roles) who travelled from town to town, setting up their stages in open places (such as inn-yards) or, with the permission of the owner, in the hall of some noble house. The touring companies continued, in the provinces, into the seventeenth century; but in London, in 1576, a new building was erected for the performance of plays. This was the Theatre, the first purpose-built playhouse in England. Other playhouses followed, including Shakespeare's own theatre, The Globe, which was completed in 1599. The English drama reached new heights of eloquence.

There were those who disapproved, of course. The theatres, which brought large crowds together, could encourage the spread of disease—and dangerous ideas. During the summer, when the plague was at its worst, the playhouses were closed. A constant censorship was imposed, more or less severe at different times. The Puritan faction tried to close down the theatres, but—partly because there was royal favour for the drama, and partly because the buildings were outside the city limits—they did not succeed until 1642.

Theatre

From contemporary comments and sketches—most particularly a drawing by a Dutch visitor, Johannes de Witt—it is possible to form some idea of the typical Elizabethan playhouse for which most of Shakespeare's plays were written. Hexagonal in shape, it had three roofed galleries encircling an open courtyard. The plain, high stage projected into the yard, where it was surrounded by the audience of standing 'groundlings'. At the back were two doors for the actors' entrances and exits; and above these doors was a balcony—useful for a musicians' gallery or for the acting of scenes *'above'*. Over the stage was a thatched roof, supported on two pillars, forming a canopy—which seems to have been painted with the sun, moon, and stars for the 'heavens'.

Underneath was space (concealed by curtaining) which could be used by characters ascending and descending through a trap-door in the stage. Costumes and properties were kept backstage, in the 'tiring house'. The actors dressed lavishly, often wearing the secondhand clothes bestowed by rich patrons. Stage properties were important for defining a location, but the dramatist's own words were needed to explain the time of day, since all performances took place in the early afternoon.

Selected Further Reading

Barber, C.L., *Shakespeare's Festive Comedy: A Study of Dramatic Form and Its Relation to Social Custom*, (Princeton, N.J., 1959).

Bradbury, M., and Palmer, D., eds, *Shakespearean Comedy*, Stratford upon Avon Studies, 14, (London, 1972).

Bradbrook, Muriel C., *The Growth and Structure of Elizabethan Comedy*, (London, 1955).

Charlton, H.B., *Shakespearian Comedy*, (London, 1938).

Evans, Bertrand, *Shakespeare's Comedies*, (Oxford, 1960).

Gardner, Helen, '*As You Like It*', in *More Talking of Shakespeare*, ed. John Garrett, (London, 1959), 17–32.

Jackson, Russell, *Perfect Types of Womanhood: Rosalind, Beatrice and Viola in Victorian Criticism and Performance*, Shakespeare Survey 32 (1979), 15–26.

Jackson, Russell, and Smallwood, Robert, eds, *Players of Shakespeare 2*, (Cambridge, 1988).

Jamieson, Michael, *Shakespeare: 'As You Like It'*, Arnold's Studies in English Literature, 25, (London, 1965).

Jenkins, Harold, '*As You Like It*', Shakespeare Survey 8, (1955), 40–51.

Lascelles, Mary, 'Shakespeare's Pastoral Comedy' in *More Talking of Shakespeare*, ed. John Garrett, (London, 1959), 70–86.

Muir, Kenneth, *Shakespeare's Comic Sequence*, (Liverpool, 1979). *The Sources of Shakespeare's Plays*, (London, 1977).

Nevo, Ruth, *Comic Transformations in Shakespeare*, (London, 1980).

Salinger, L.G., *Shakespeare and the Traditions of Comedy*, (Cambridge, 1974).

Background Reading

Blake, N.F., *Shakespeare's Language: an Introduction*, (Methuen, 1983).

Muir, K., and Schoenbaum, S., *A New Companion to Shakespeare Studies*, (Cambridge, 1971).

Schoenbaum, S., *William Shakespeare: A Documentary Life*, (Oxford, 1975).

Thomson, Peter, *Shakespeare's Theatre*, (Routledge and Kegan Paul, 1983).

William Shakespeare, 1564–1616

Elizabeth I was Queen of England when Shakespeare was born in
1564. He was the son of a tradesman who made and sold gloves in
the small town of Stratford-upon-Avon, and he was educated at the
grammar school in that town. Shakespeare did not go to university
when he left school, but worked, perhaps, in his father's business.
When he was eighteen he married Anne Hathaway, who became
the mother of his daughter, Susanna, in 1583, and of twins in 1585.

There is nothing exciting, or even unusual, in this story; and
from 1585 until 1592 there are no documents that can tell us
anything at all about Shakespeare. But we have learned that in 1592
he was known in London, and that he had become both an actor
and a playwright.

We do not know when Shakespeare wrote his first play, and
indeed we are not sure of the order in which he wrote his works. If
you look on page 122 at the list of his writings and their approxi-
mate dates, you will see how he started by writing plays on subjects
taken from the history of England. No doubt this was partly
because he was always an intensely patriotic man—but he was also
a very shrewd business-man. He could see that the theatre
audiences enjoyed being shown their own history, and it was certain
that he would make a profit from this kind of drama.

The plays in the next group are mainly comedies, with
romantic love stories of young people who fall in love with one
another, and at the end of the play marry and live happily ever
after.

At the end of the sixteenth century the happiness disappears,
and Shakespeare's plays become melancholy, bitter, and tragic.
This change may have been caused by some sadness in the writer's
life (one of his twins died in 1596). Shakespeare, however, was not
the only writer whose works at this time were very serious. The
whole of England was facing a crisis. Queen Elizabeth I was
growing old. She was greatly loved, and the people were sad to
think she must soon die; they were also afraid, for the Queen had
never married, and so there was no child to succeed her.

When James I came to the throne in 1603, Shakespeare
continued to write serious drama—the great tragedies and the plays
based on Roman history (such as *Julius Caesar*) for which he is most

famous. Finally, before he retired from the theatre, he wrote another set of comedies. These all have the same theme: they tell of happiness which is lost, and then found again.

Shakespeare returned from London to Stratford, his home town. He was rich and successful, and he owned one of the biggest houses in the town. He died in 1616.

Shakespeare also wrote two long poems, and a collection of sonnets. The sonnets describe two love-affairs, but we do not know who the lovers were. Although there are many public documents concerned with his career as a writer and a business-man, Shakespeare has hidden his personal life from us. A nineteenth-century poet, Matthew Arnold, addressed Shakespeare in a poem, and wrote 'We ask and ask—Thou smilest, and art still'.

There is not even a trustworthy portrait of the world's greatest dramatist.

Approximate order of composition of Shakespeare's works

Period	Comedies	History plays	Tragedies	Poems
I	Comedy of Errors	Henry VI, part 1	Titus Andronicus	
	Taming of the Shrew	Henry VI, part 2		
1594	Two Gentlemen of Verona	Henry VI, part 3		Venus and Adonis
		Richard III		Rape of Lucrece
	Love's Labour's Lost	King John		
II	Midsummer Night's Dream	Richard II	Romeo and Juliet	Sonnets
	Merchant of Venice	Henry IV, part 1		
1599	Merry Wives of Windsor	Henry IV, part 2		
	Much Ado About Nothing			
	As You Like It	Henry V		
III	Twelfth Night		Julius Caesar	
	Troilus and Cressida		Hamlet	
1608	Measure for Measure		Othello	
	All's Well That Ends Well		Timon of Athens	
			King Lear	
			Macbeth	
			Antony and Cleopatra	
			Coriolanus	
IV	Pericles			
	Cymbeline			
1613	The Winter's Tale	Henry VIII		
	The Tempest			